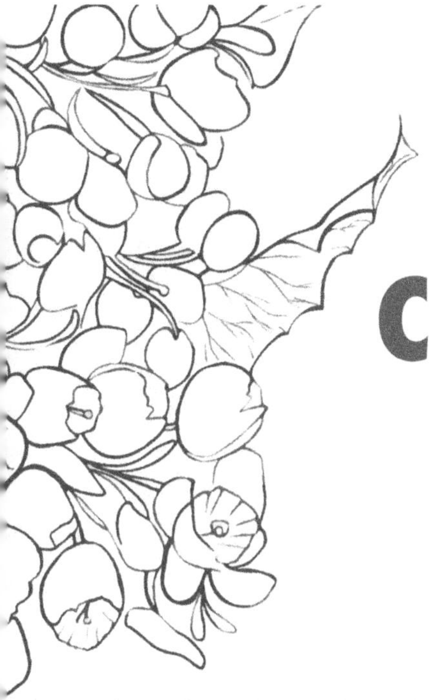

Color The World

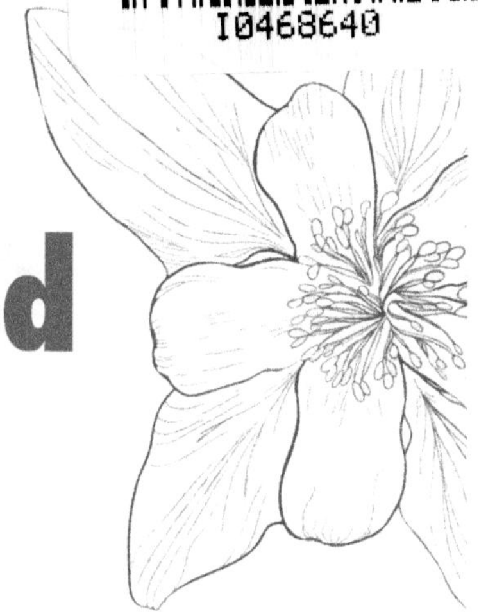

Adult Coloring Book

United States Book I

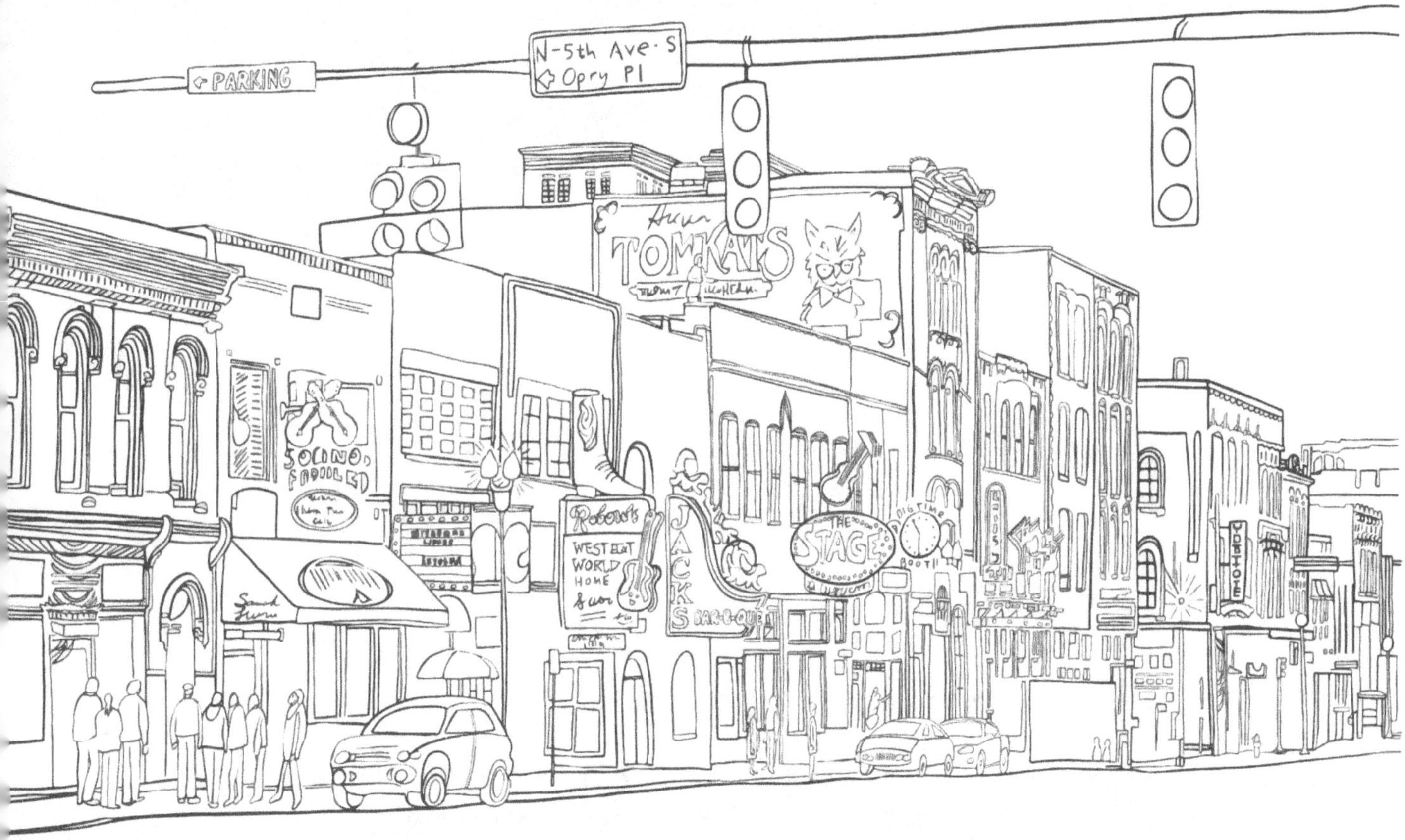

Nashville Tennessee

Original Art by **Marian Nixon**

35+ coloring pages of US scenes & state flowers

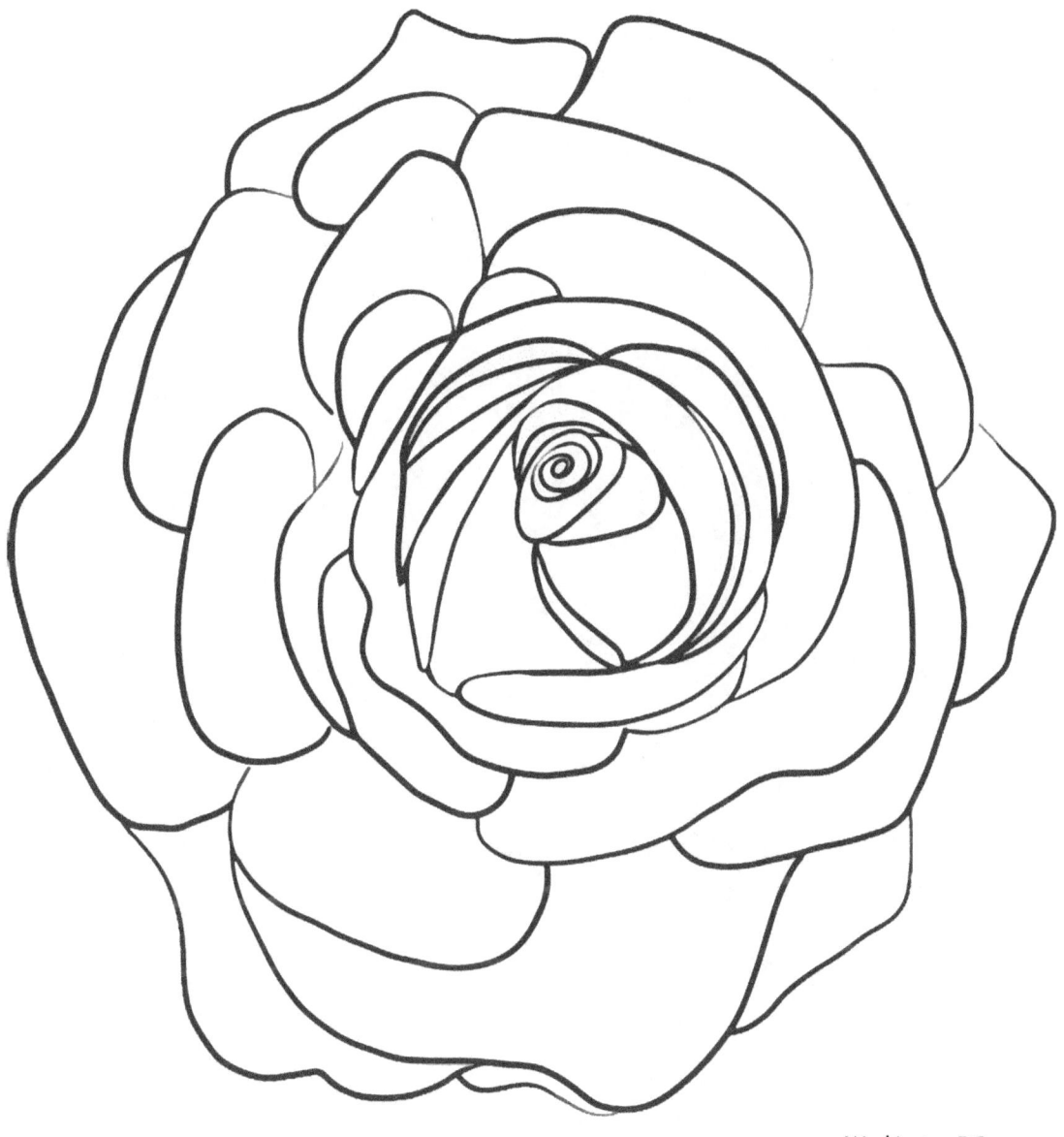

Washington DC
Rose

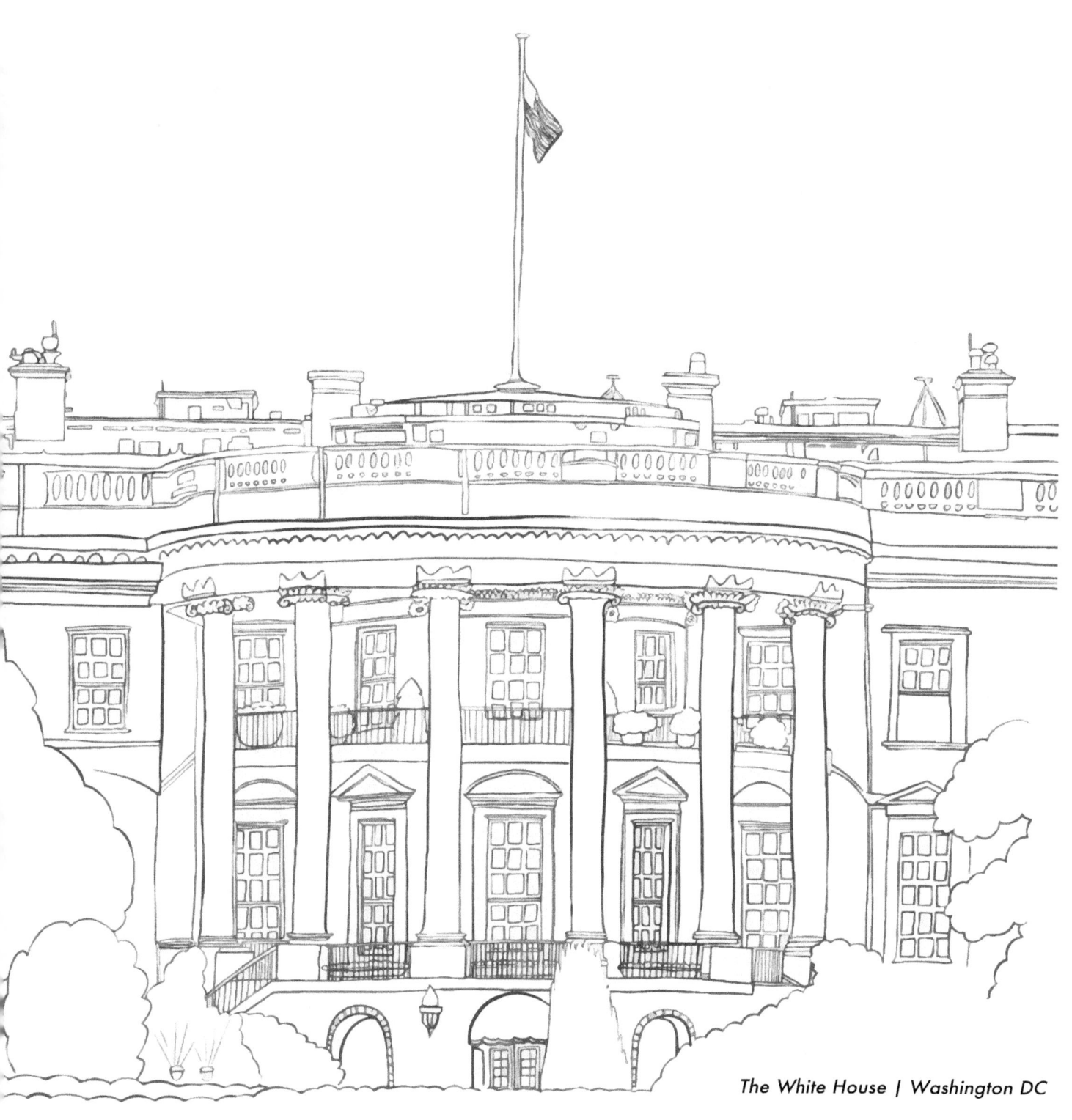

The White House | Washington DC

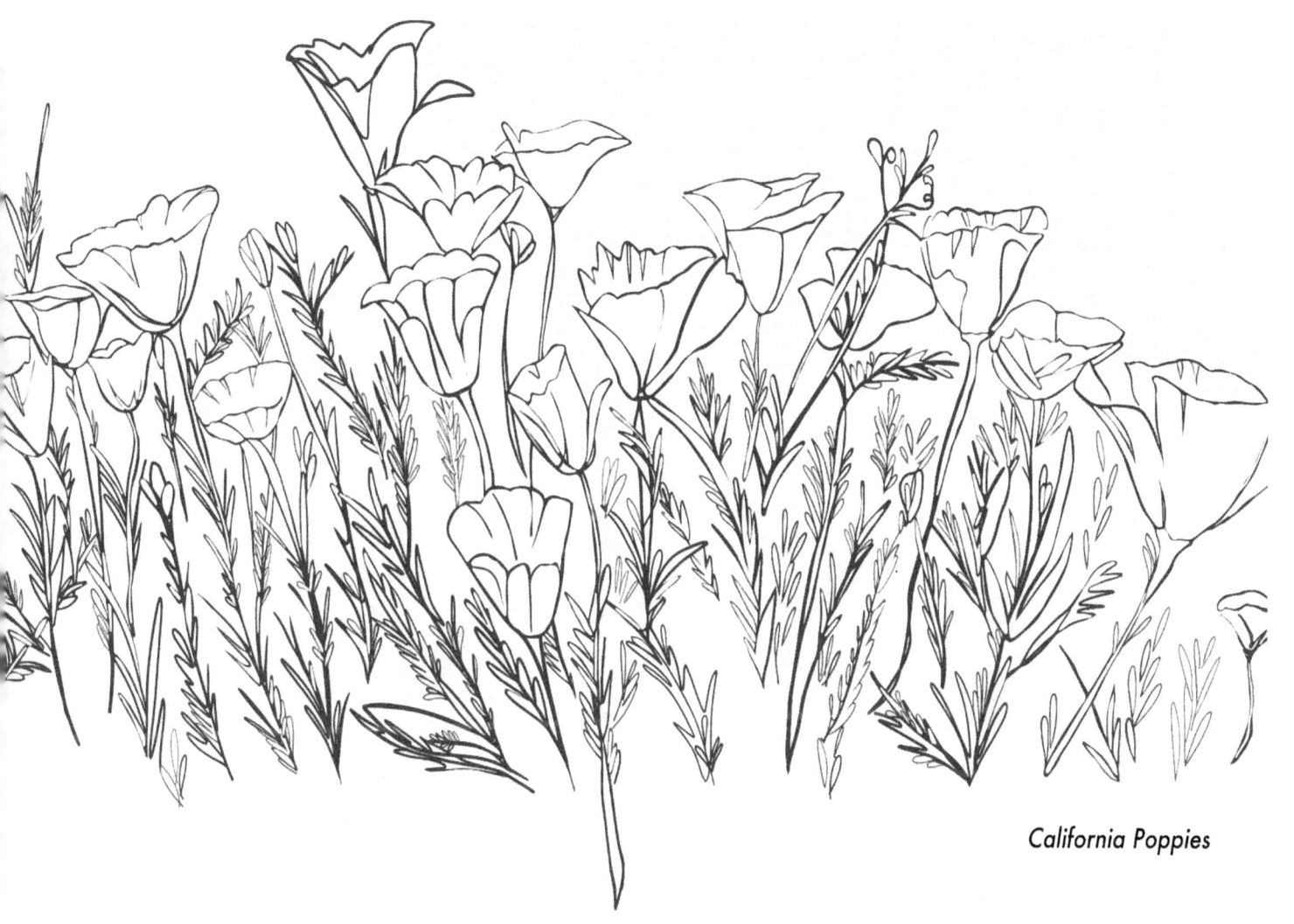

California Poppies

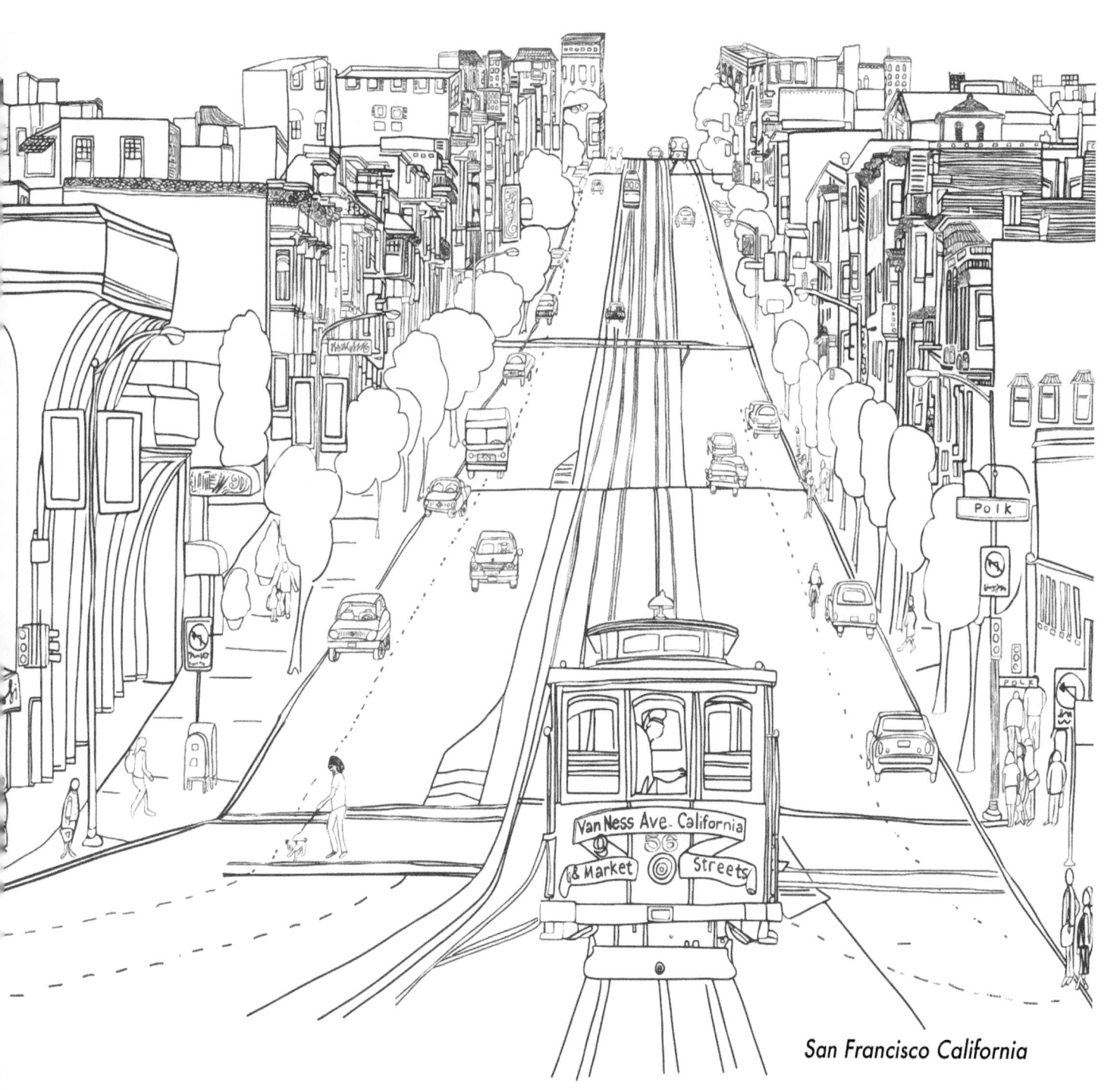

Van Ness Ave. California
56
& Market Streets

Polk

San Francisco California

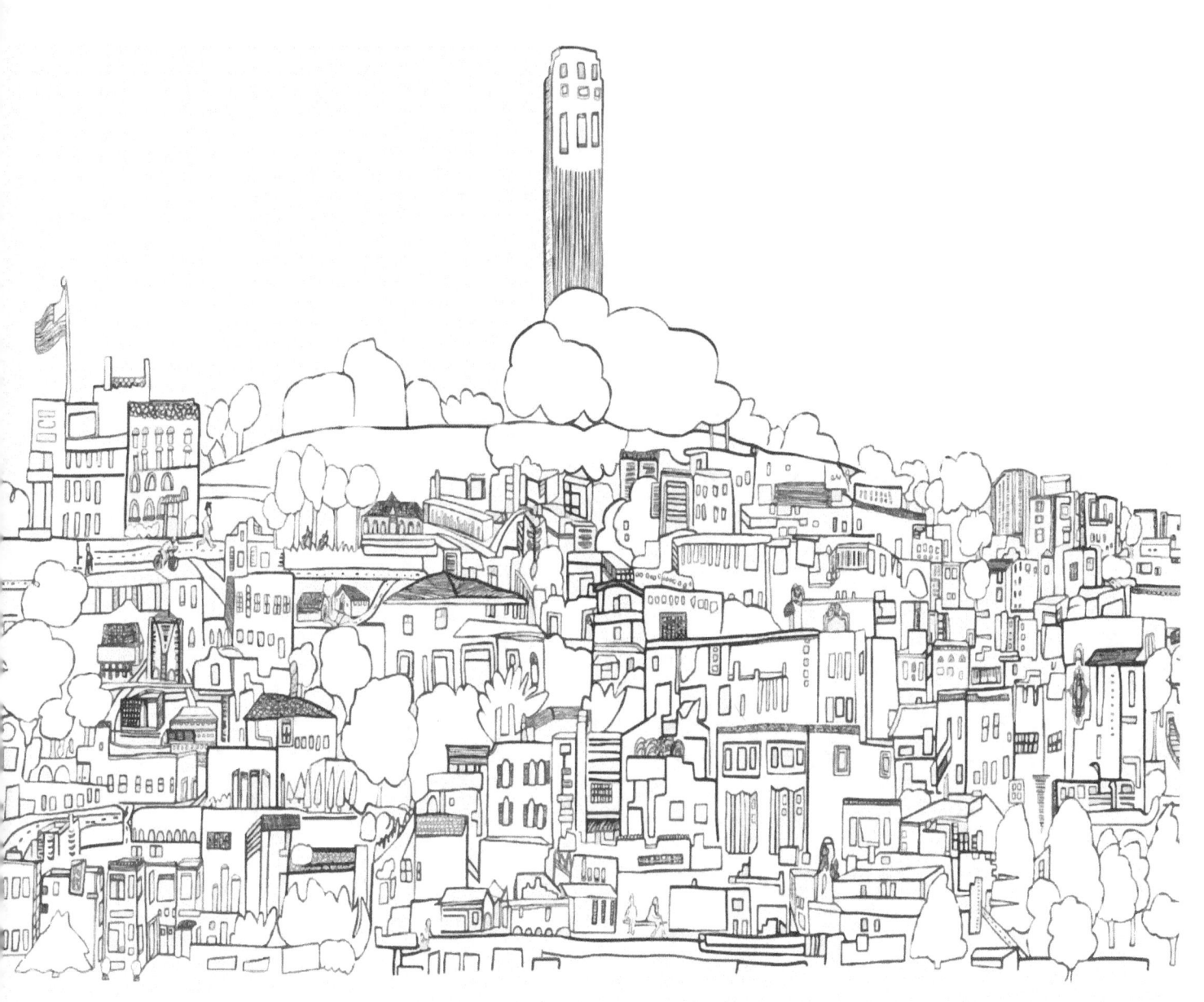

San Francisco California

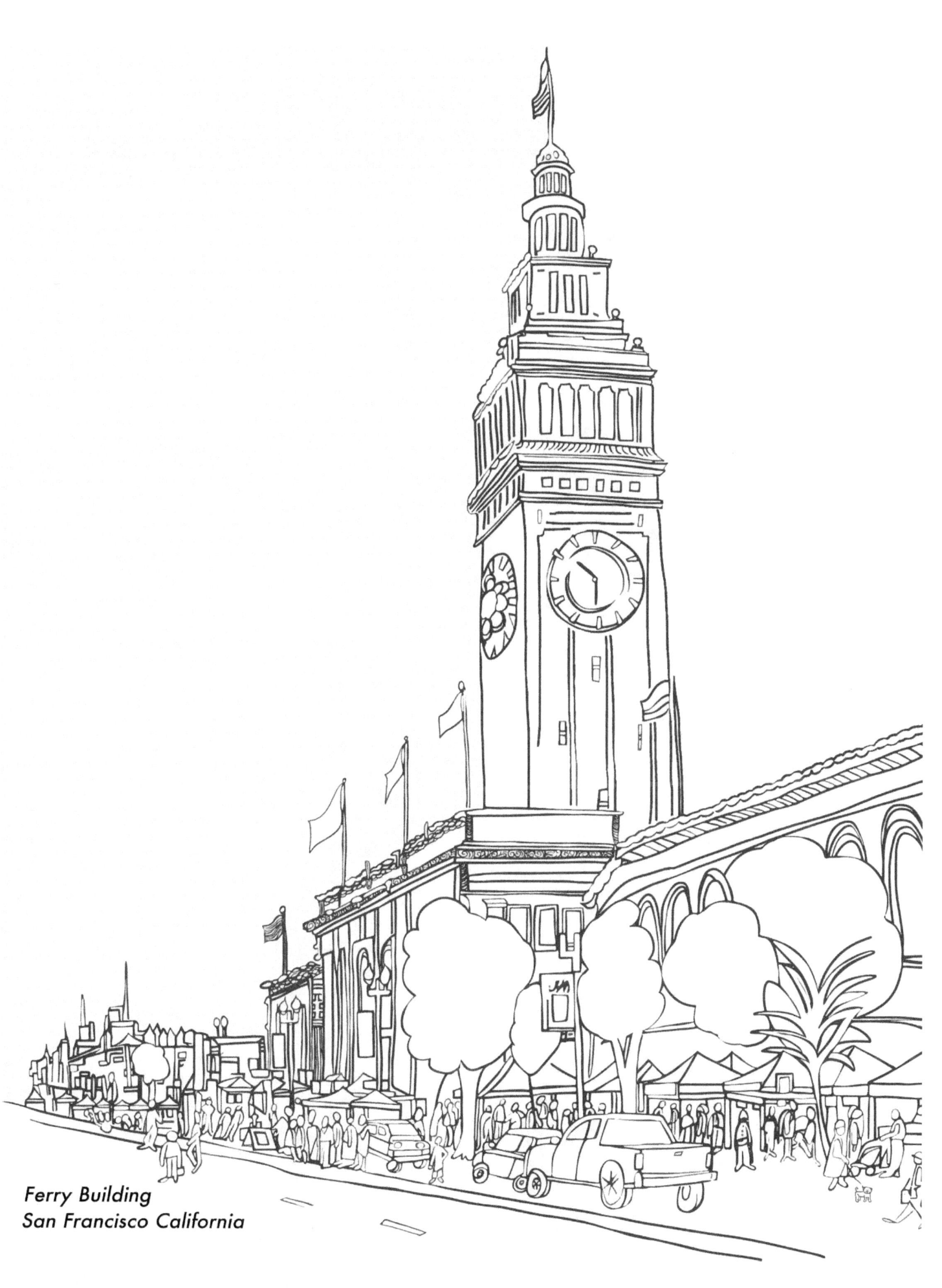

Ferry Building
San Francisco California

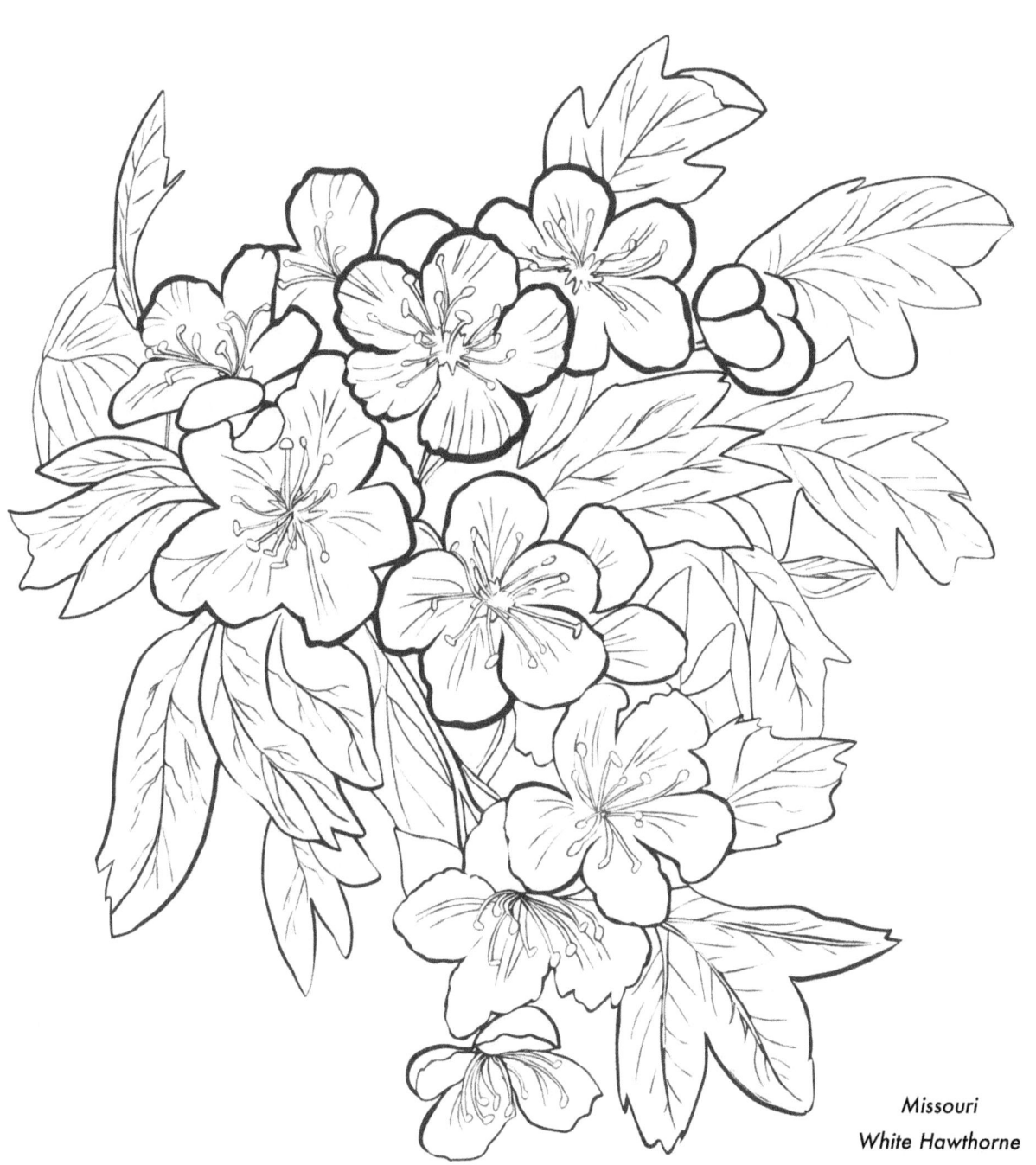

Missouri
White Hawthorne

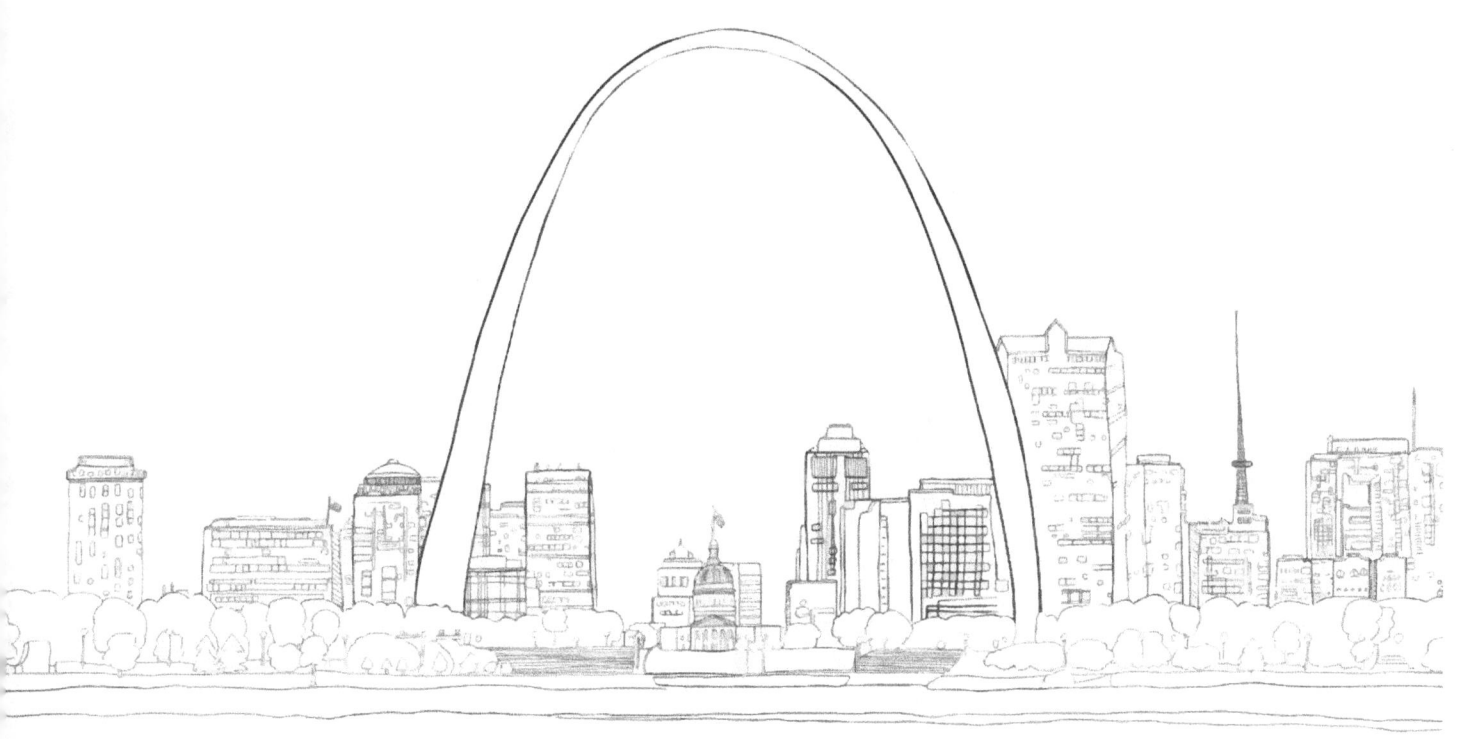

St. Louis Missouri

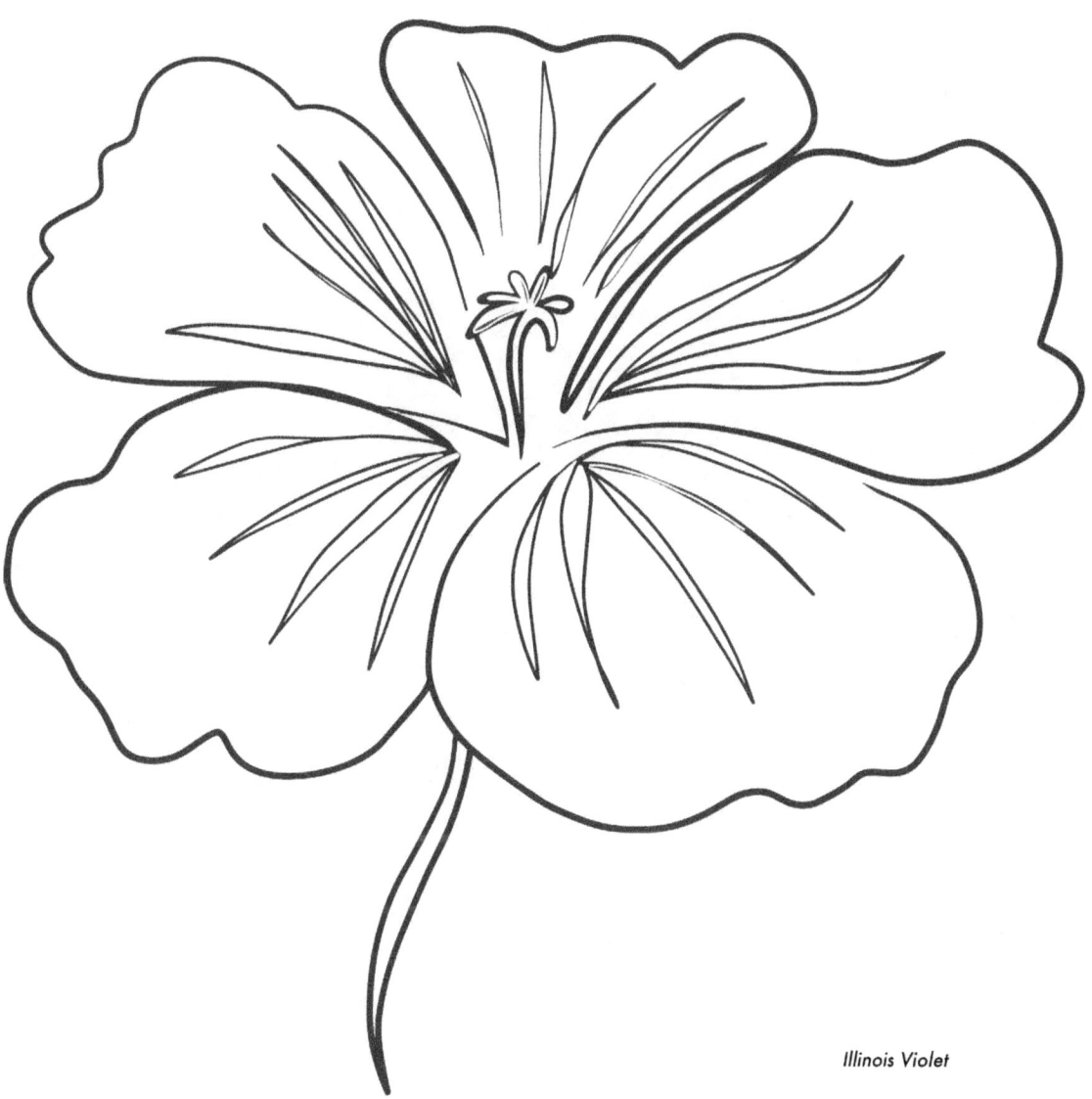

Illinois Violet

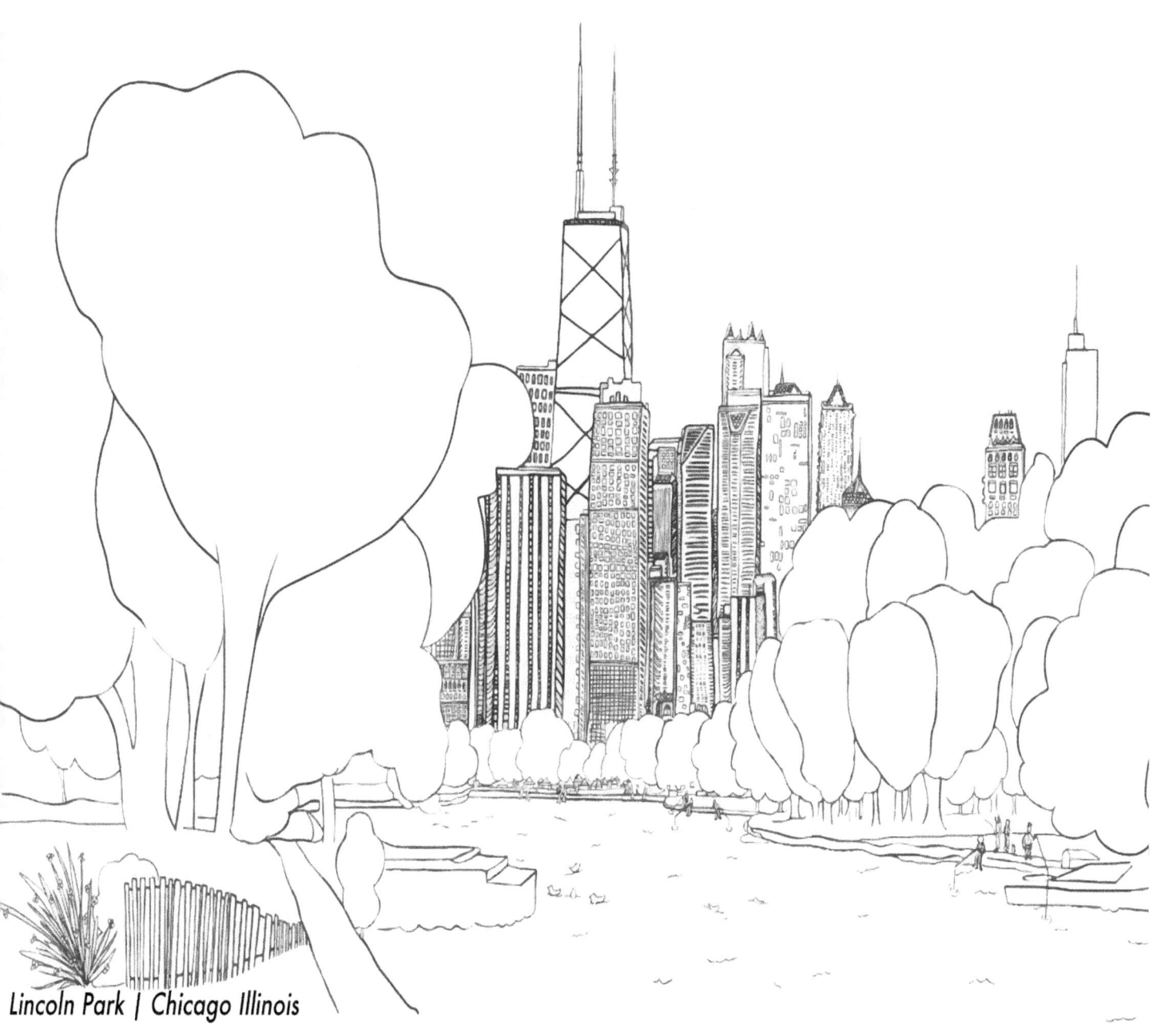

Lincoln Park | Chicago Illinois

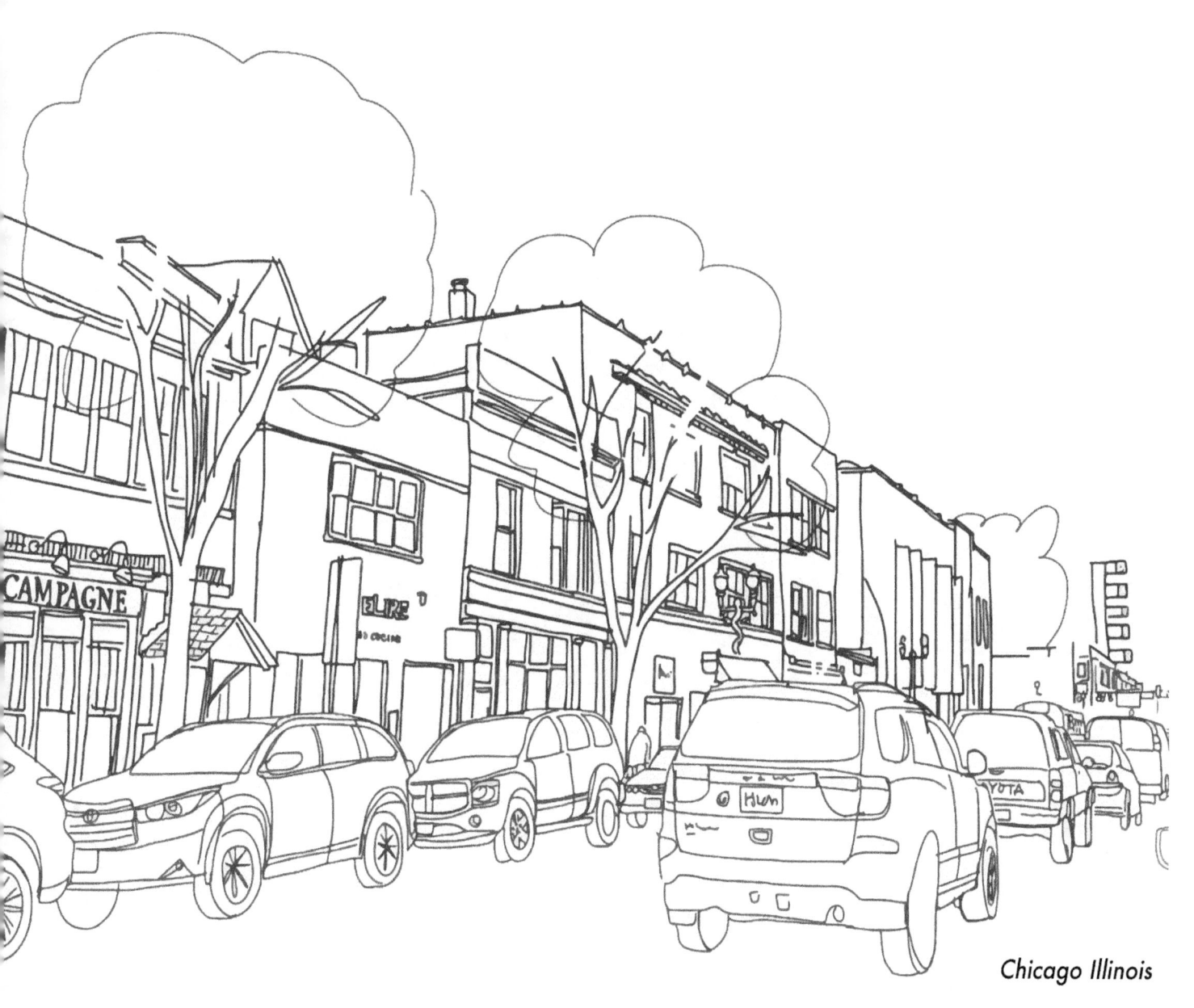

Chicago Illinois

The Art Institute | Chicago Illinois

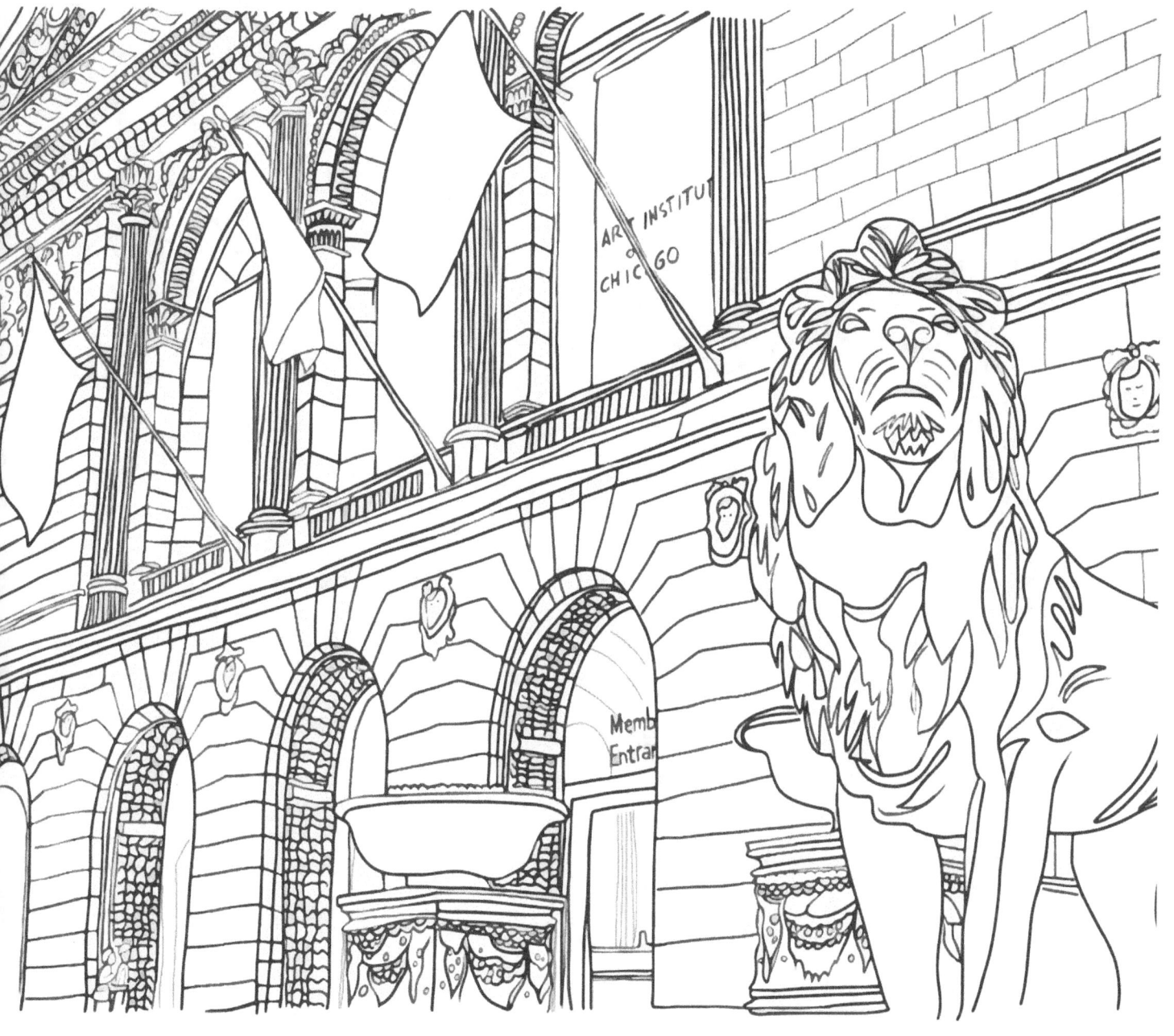

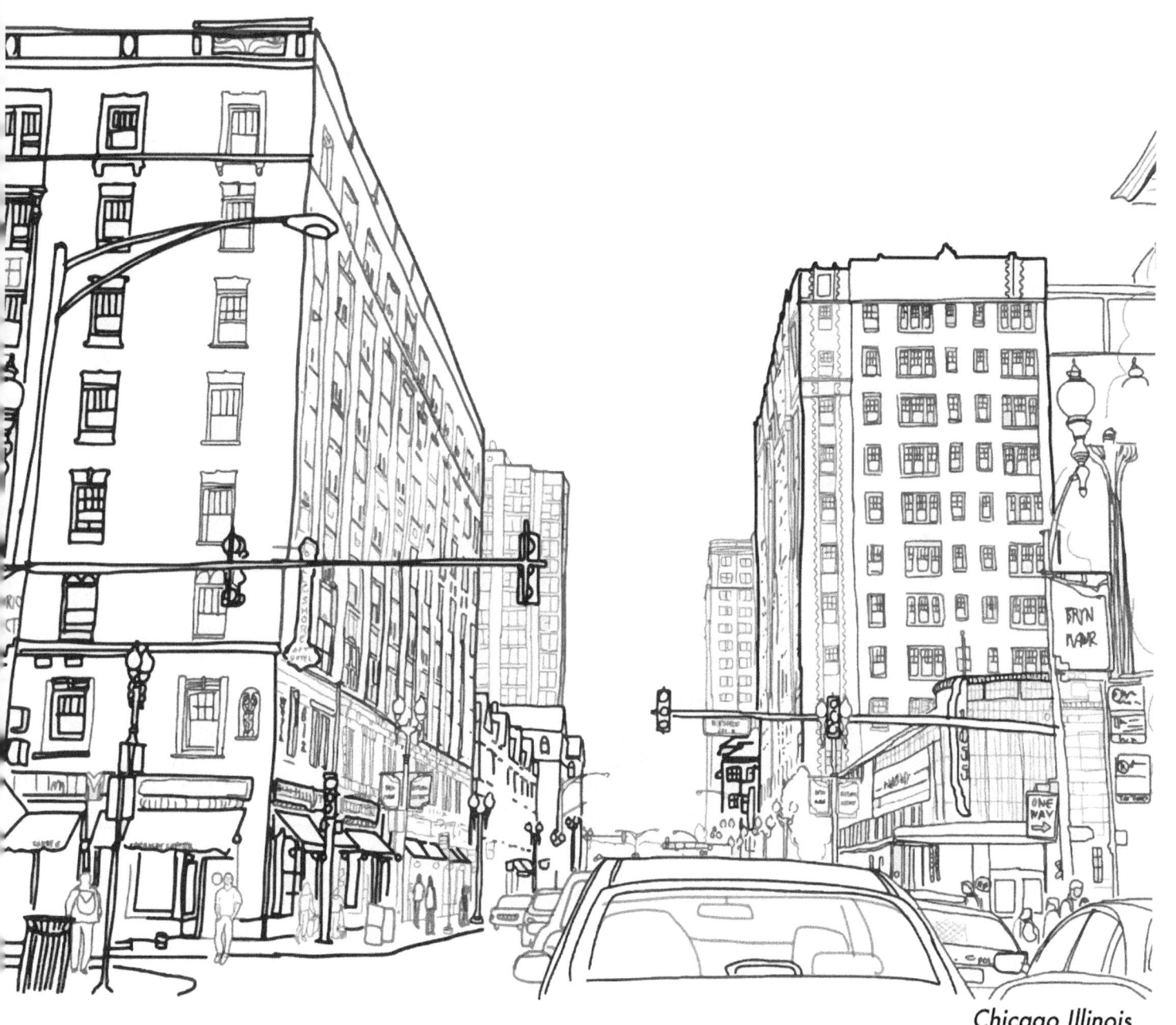

Chicago Illinois

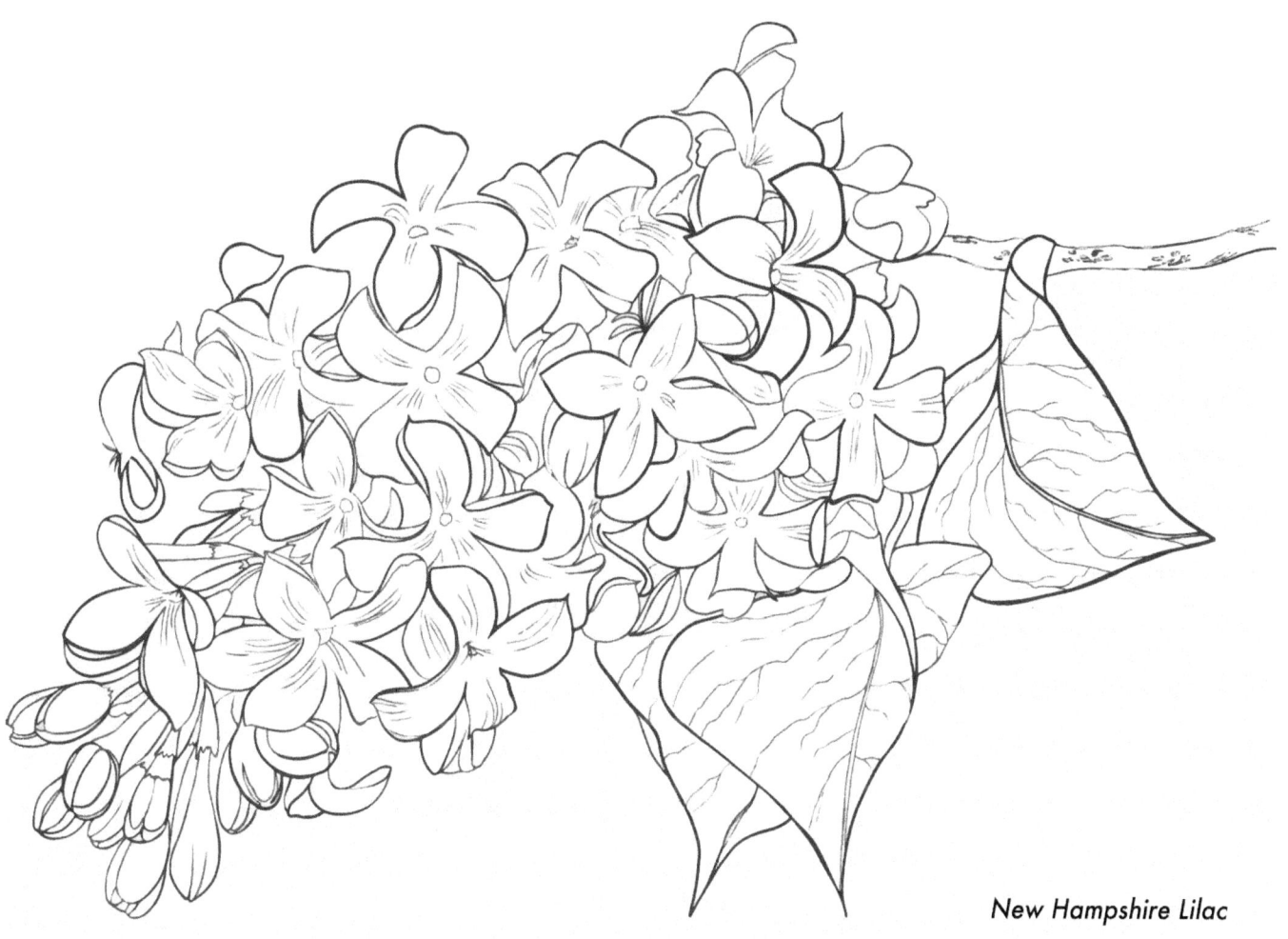

New Hampshire Lilac

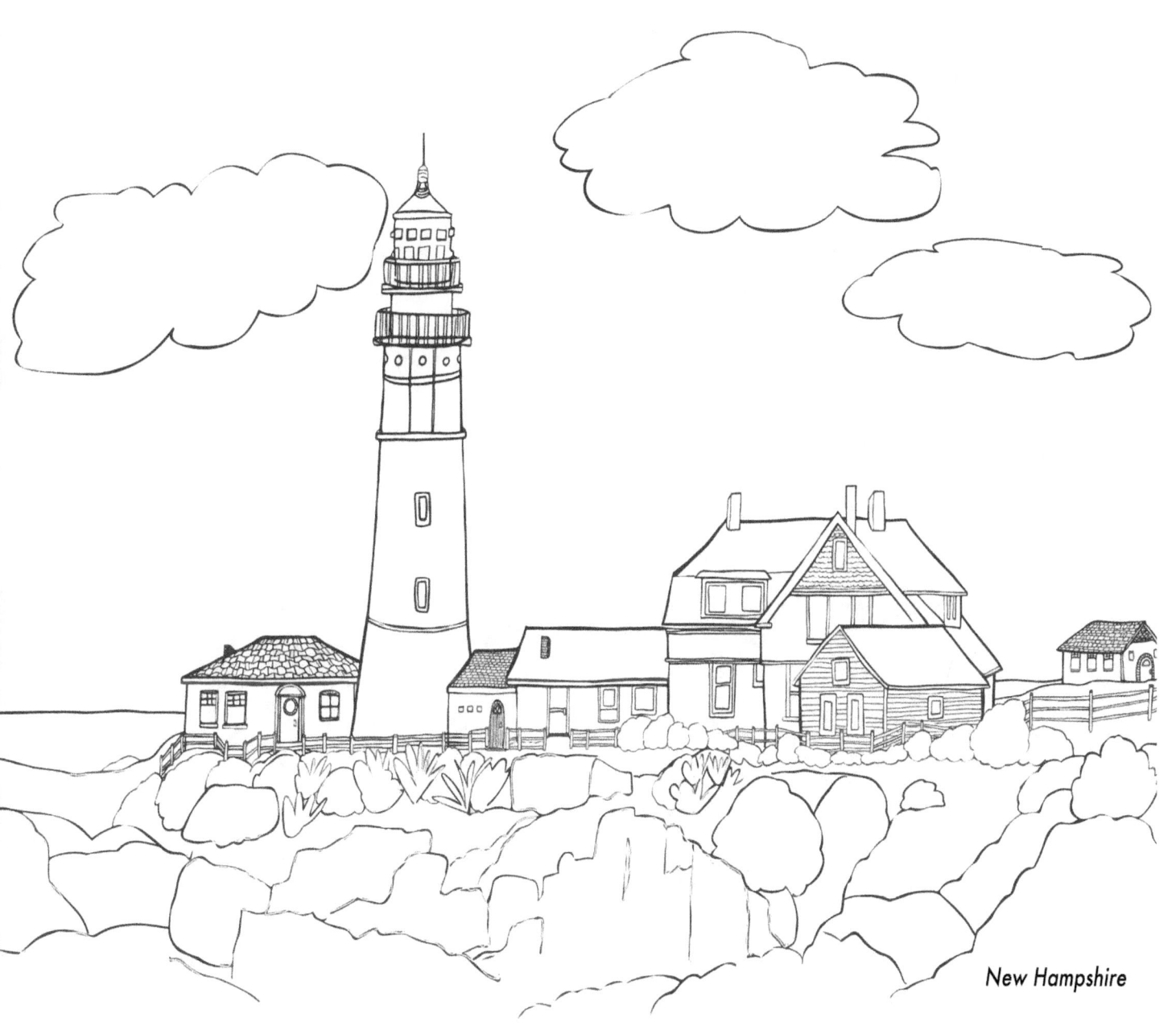

New Hampshire

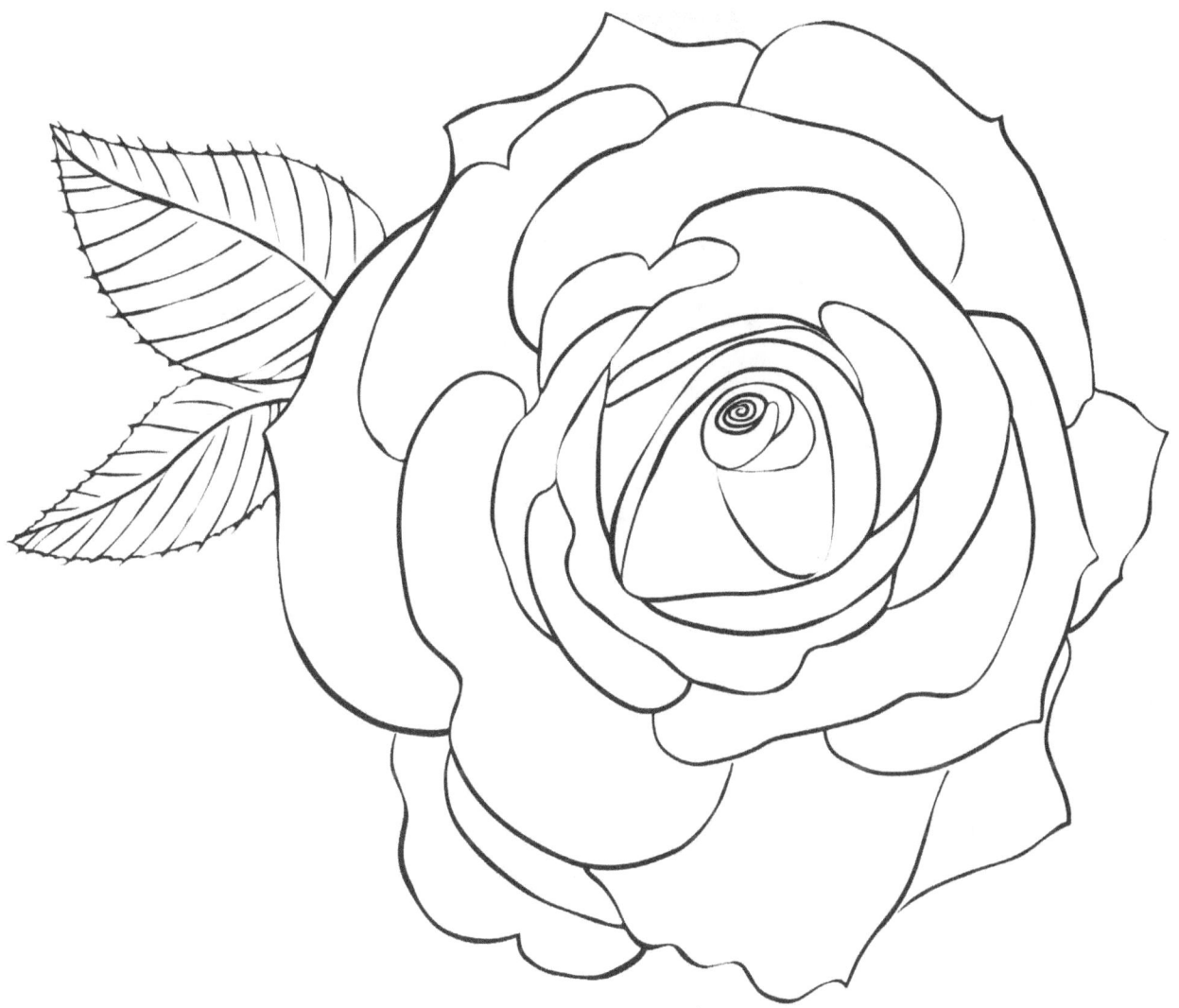

New York
Rose

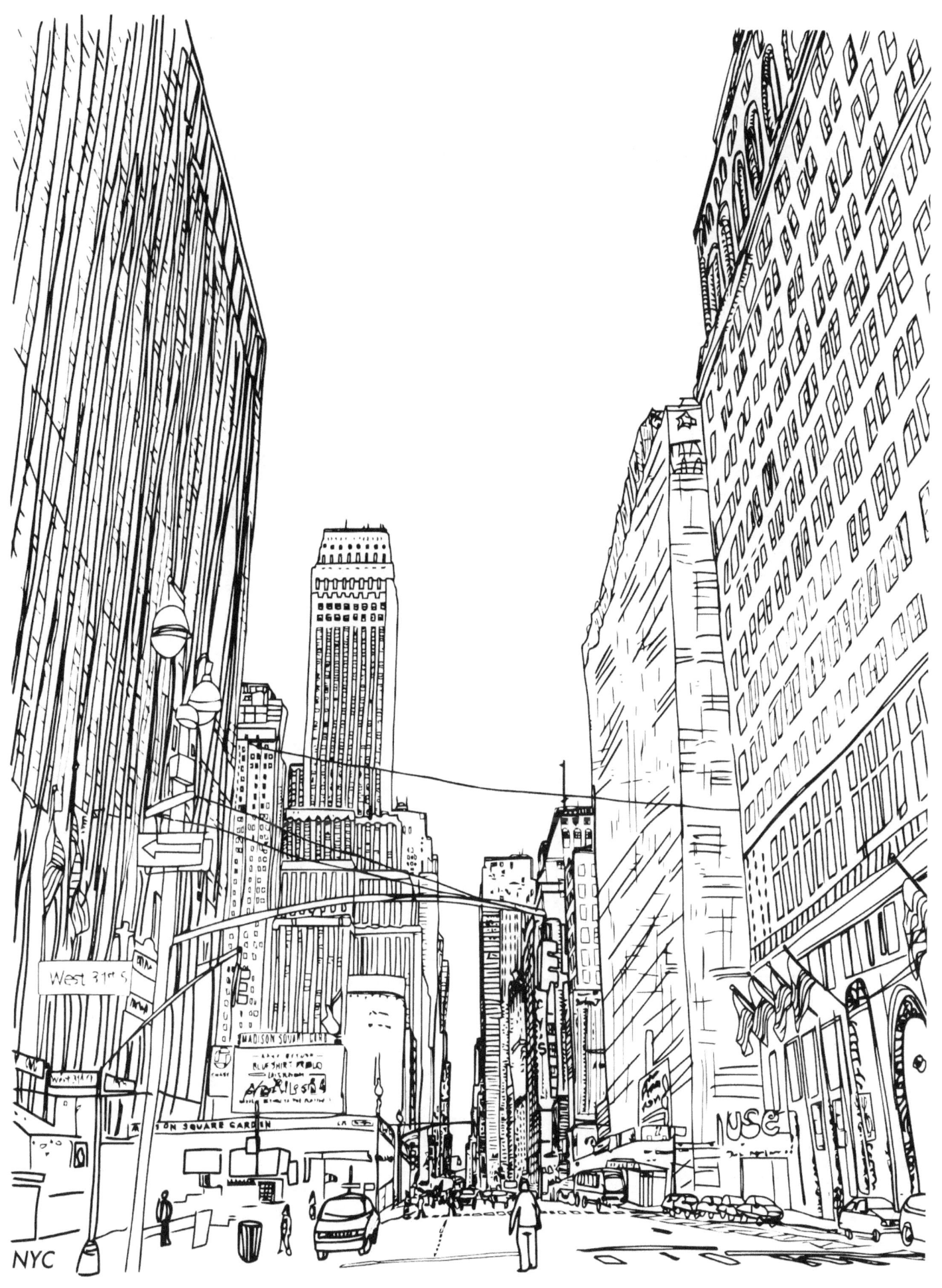

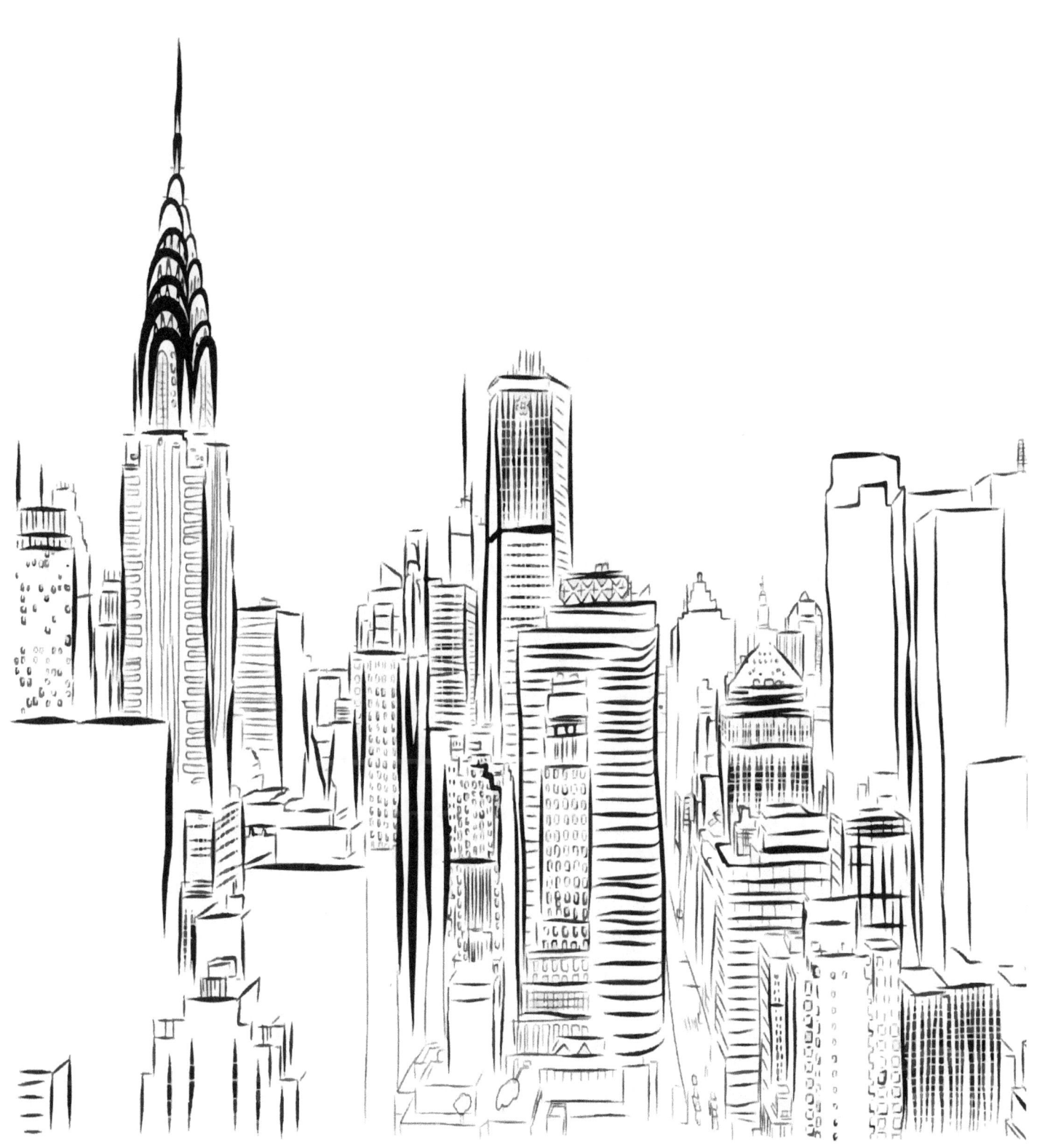

New York Skyline

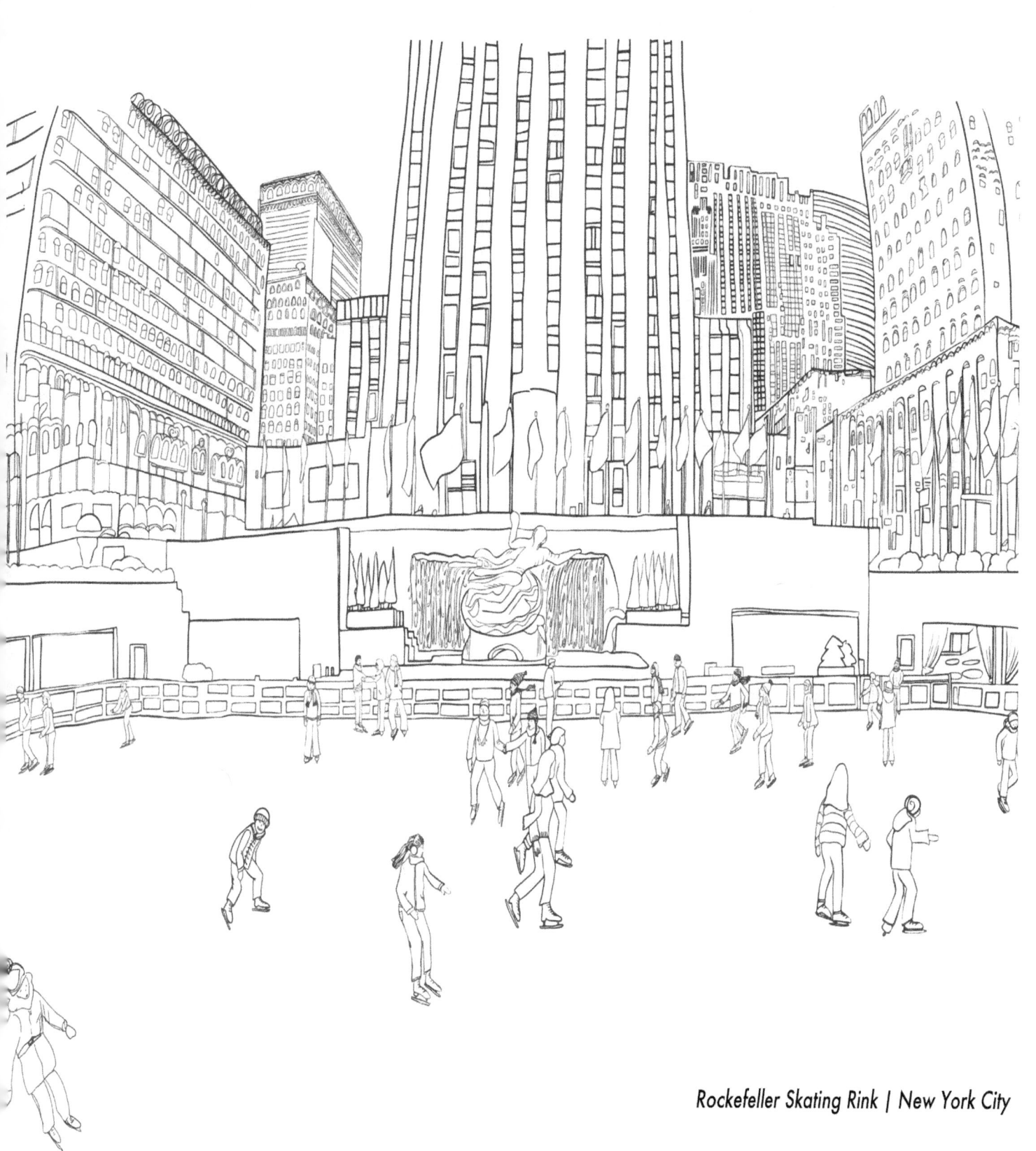

Rockefeller Skating Rink | New York City

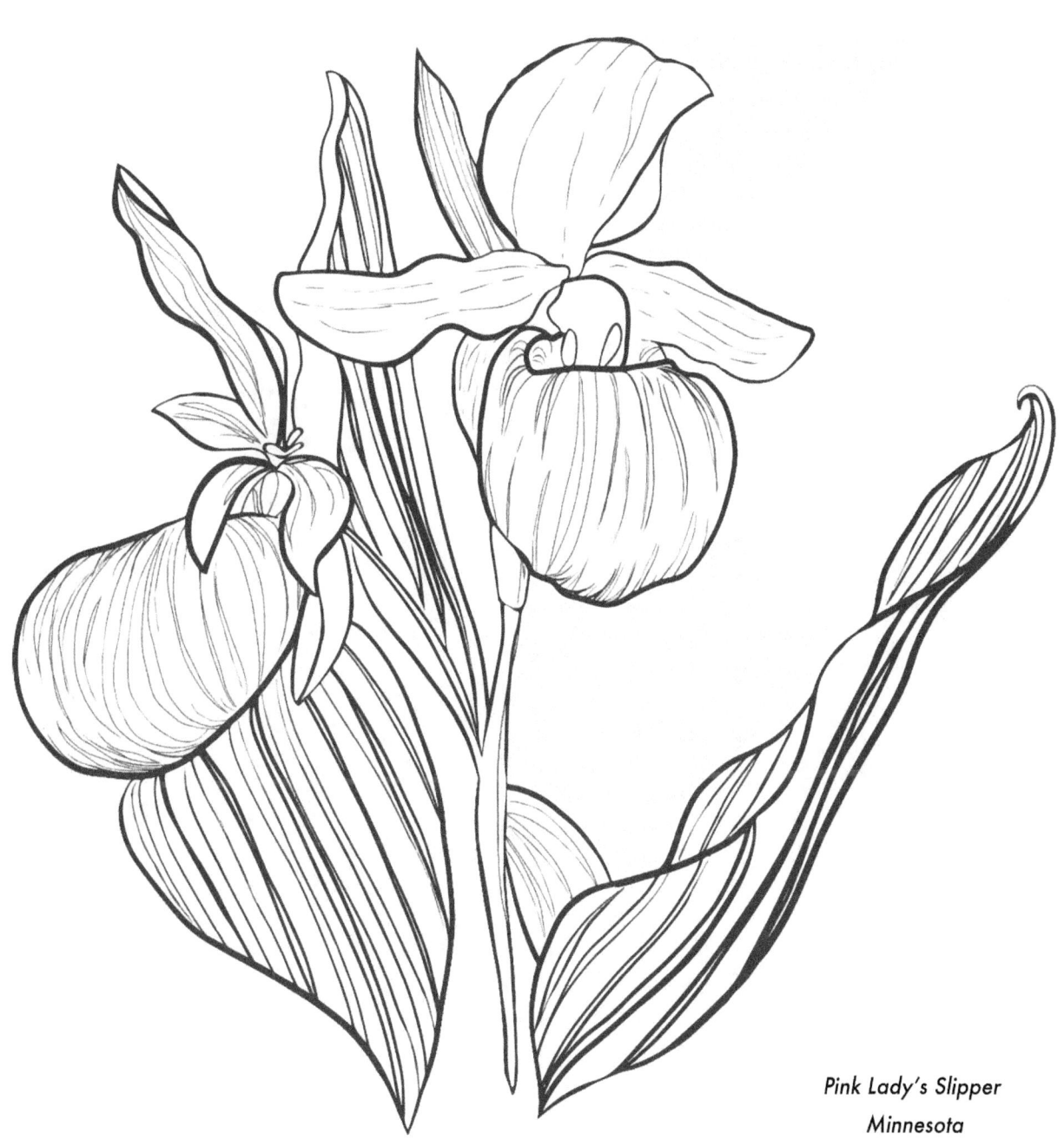

Pink Lady's Slipper
Minnesota

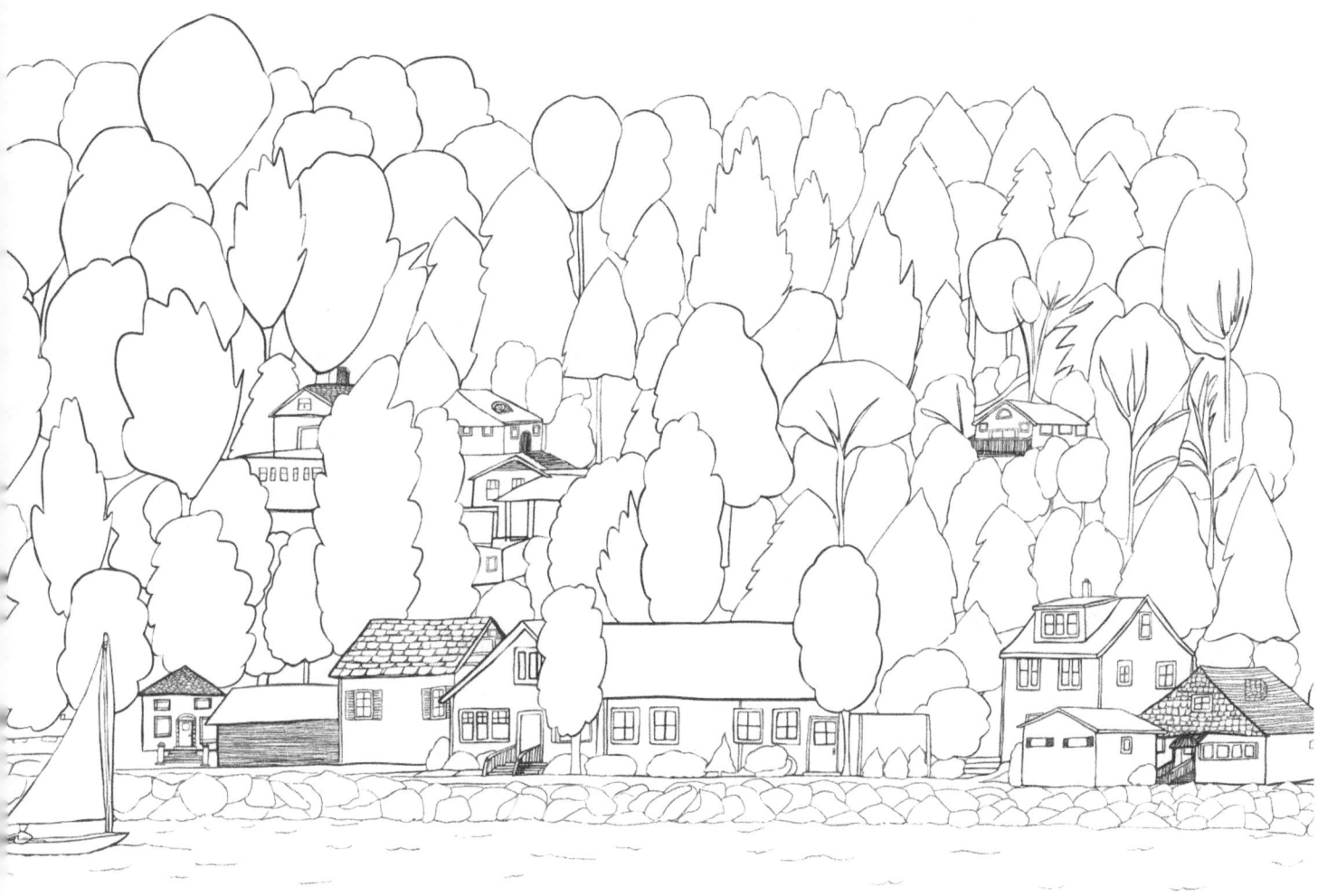

Minnesota

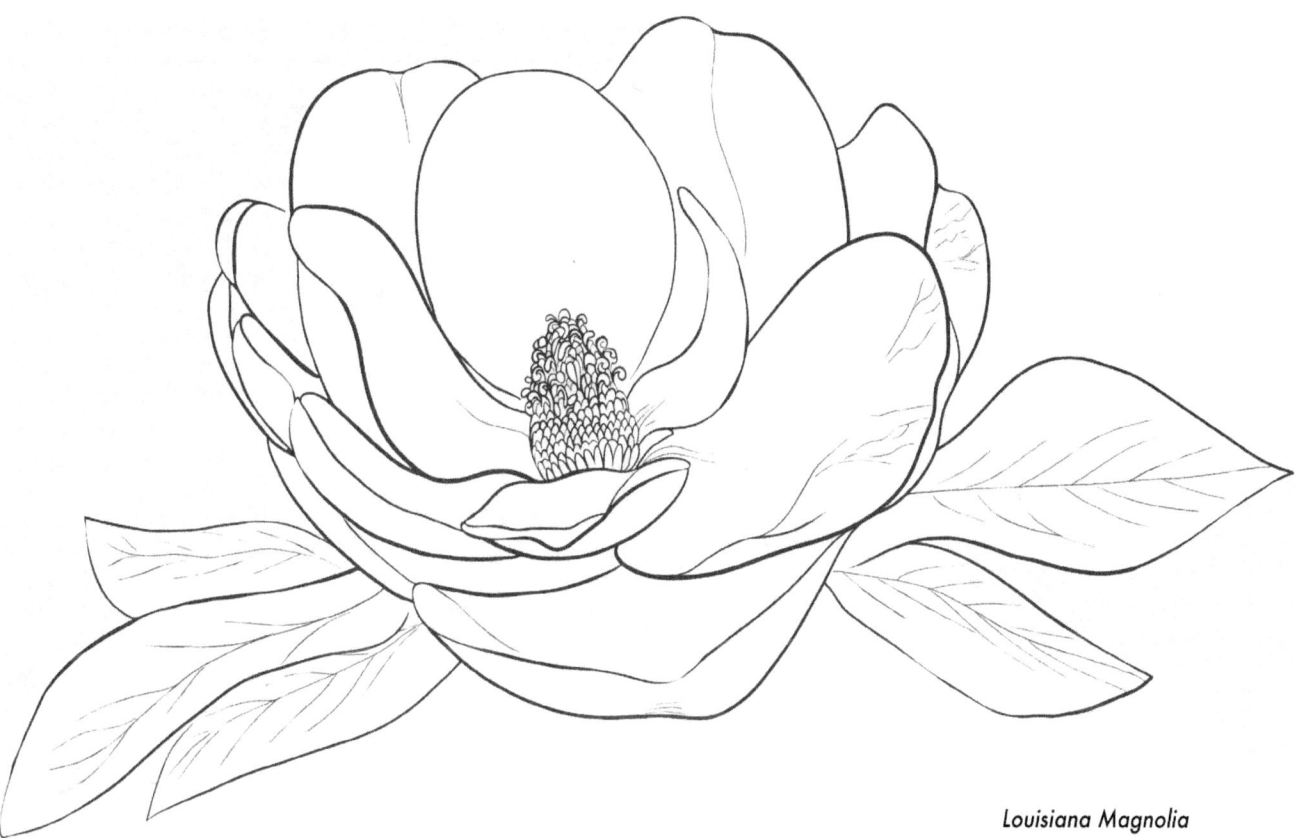

Louisiana Magnolia

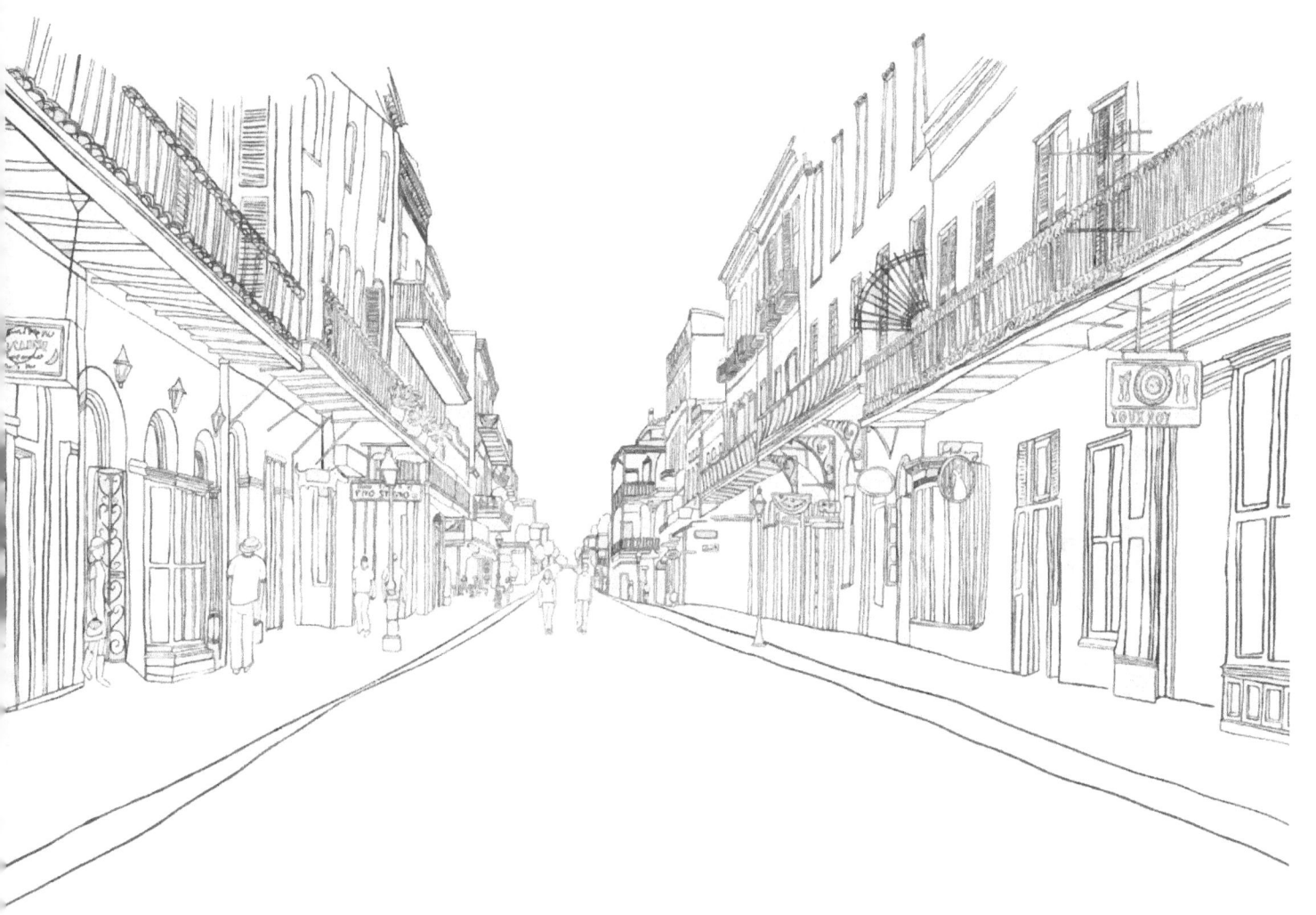

New Orleans Louisiana

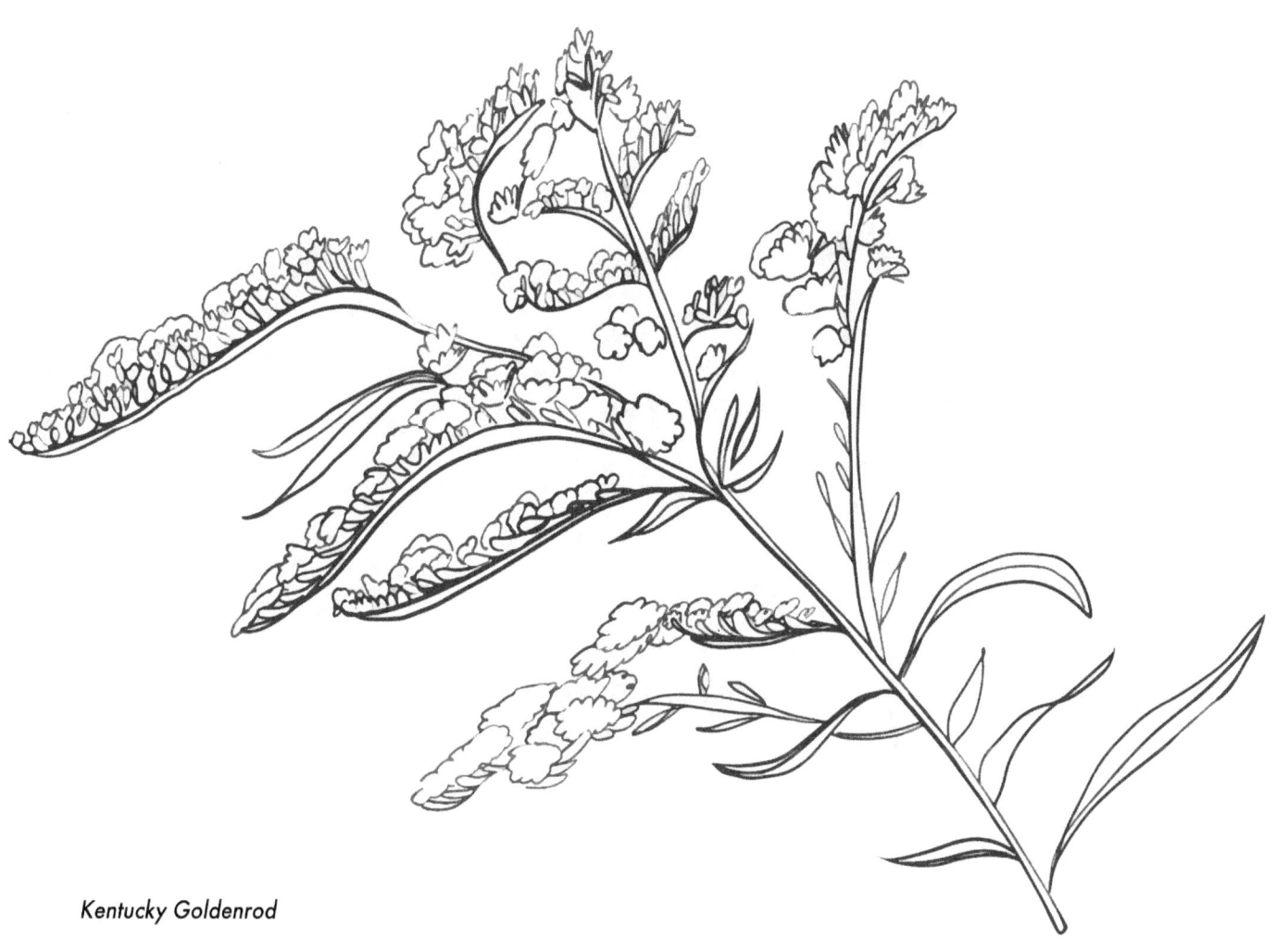

Kentucky Goldenrod

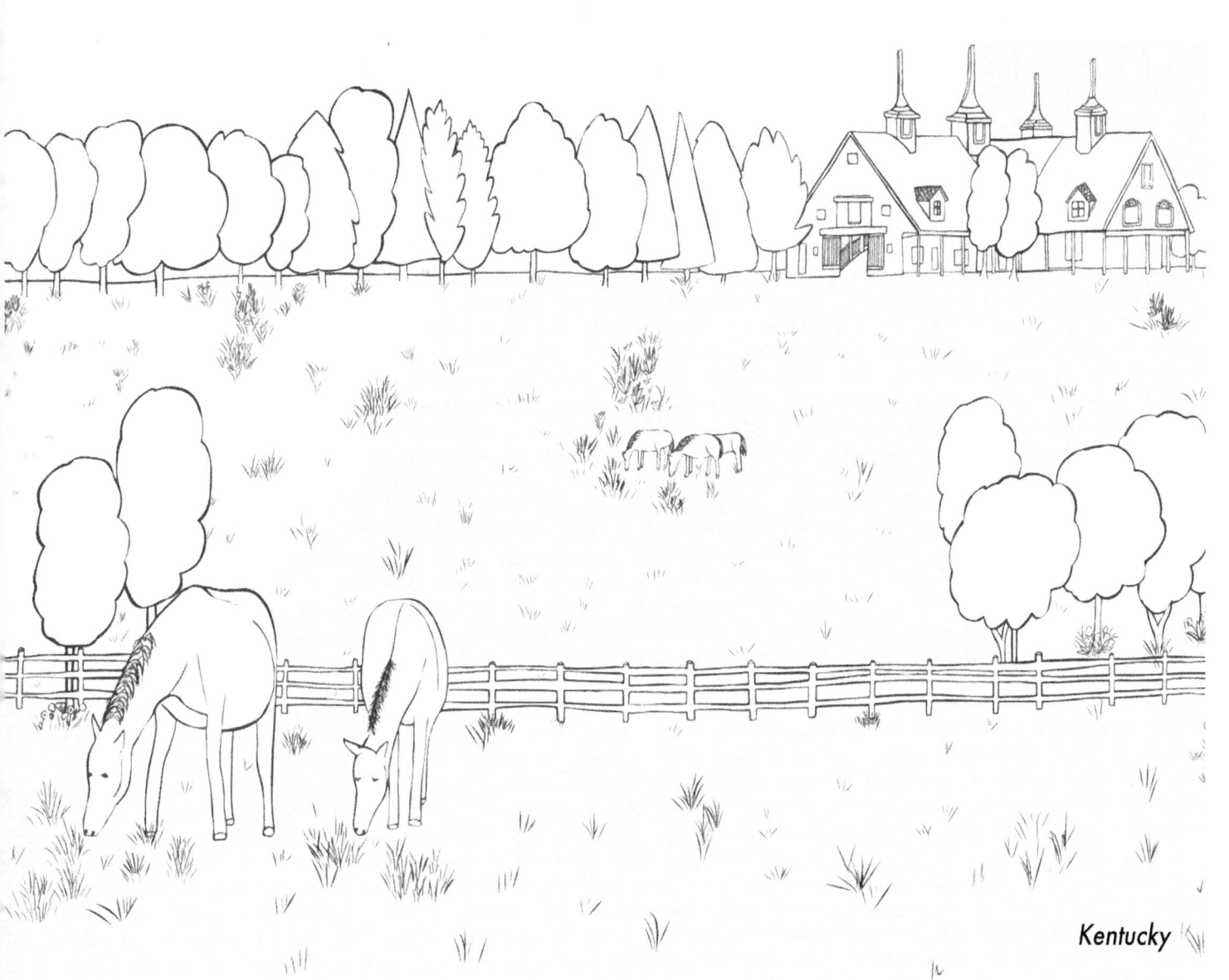

Kentucky

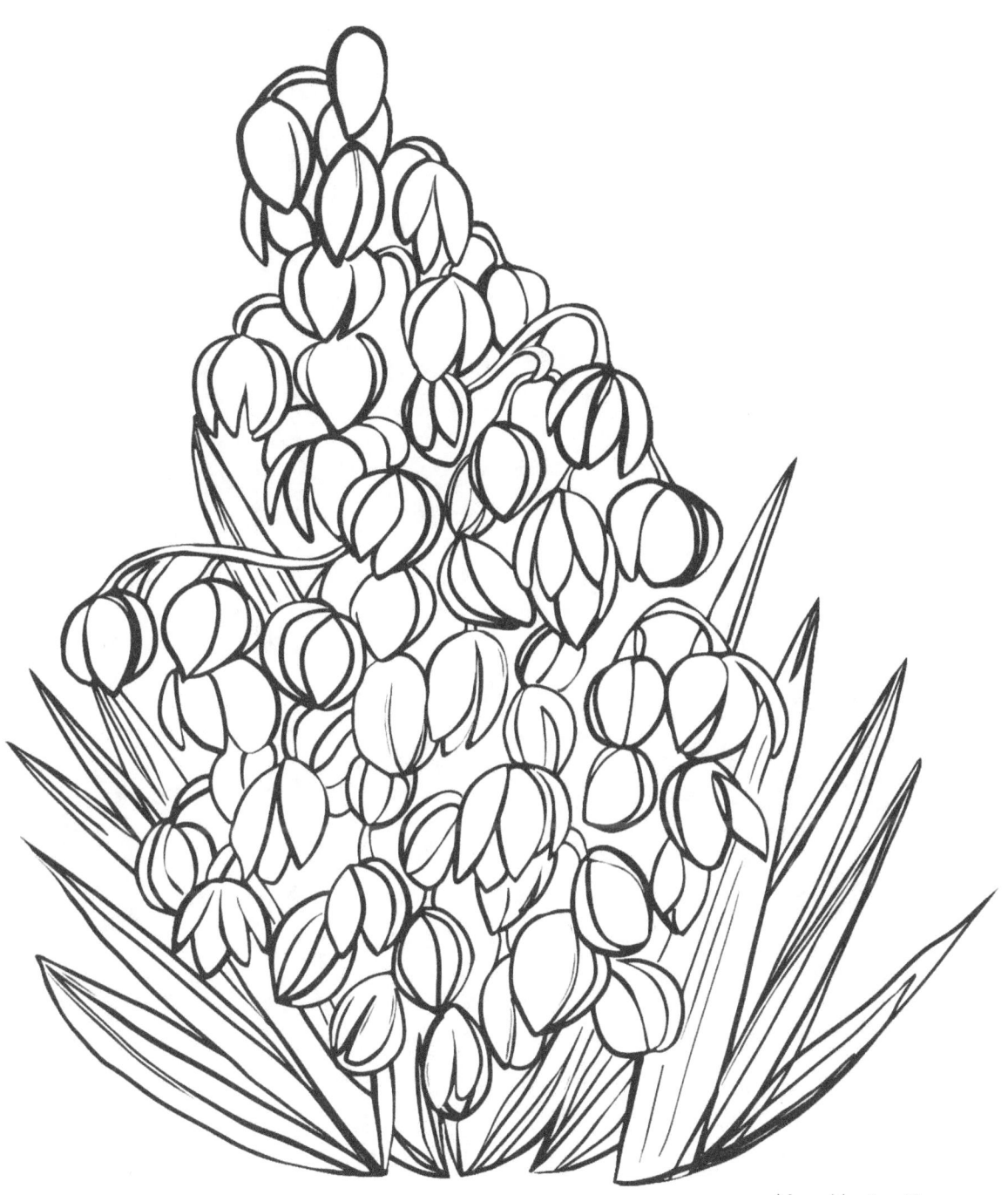

New Mexico Yucca

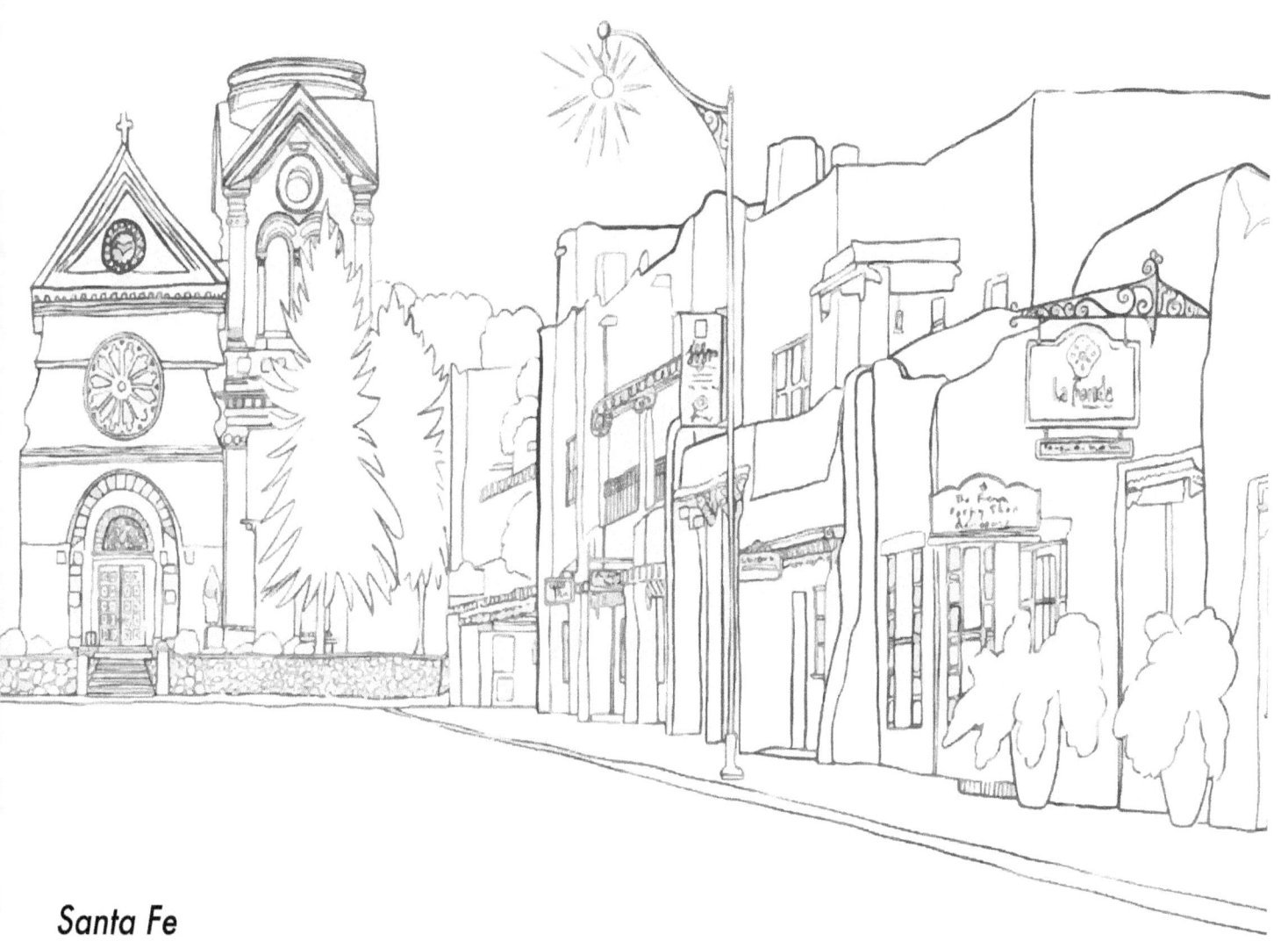

Santa Fe

New Mexico

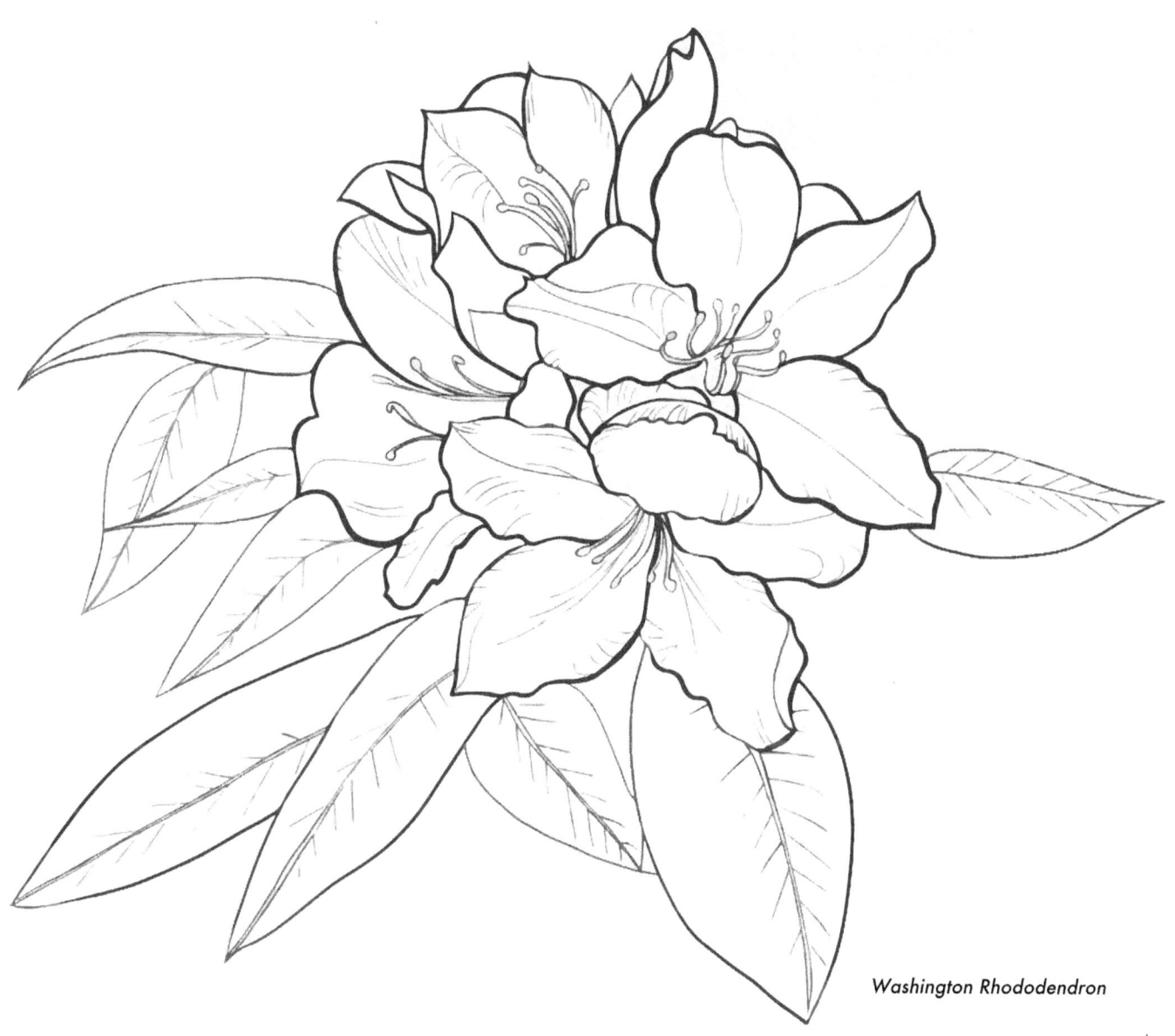

Washington Rhododendron

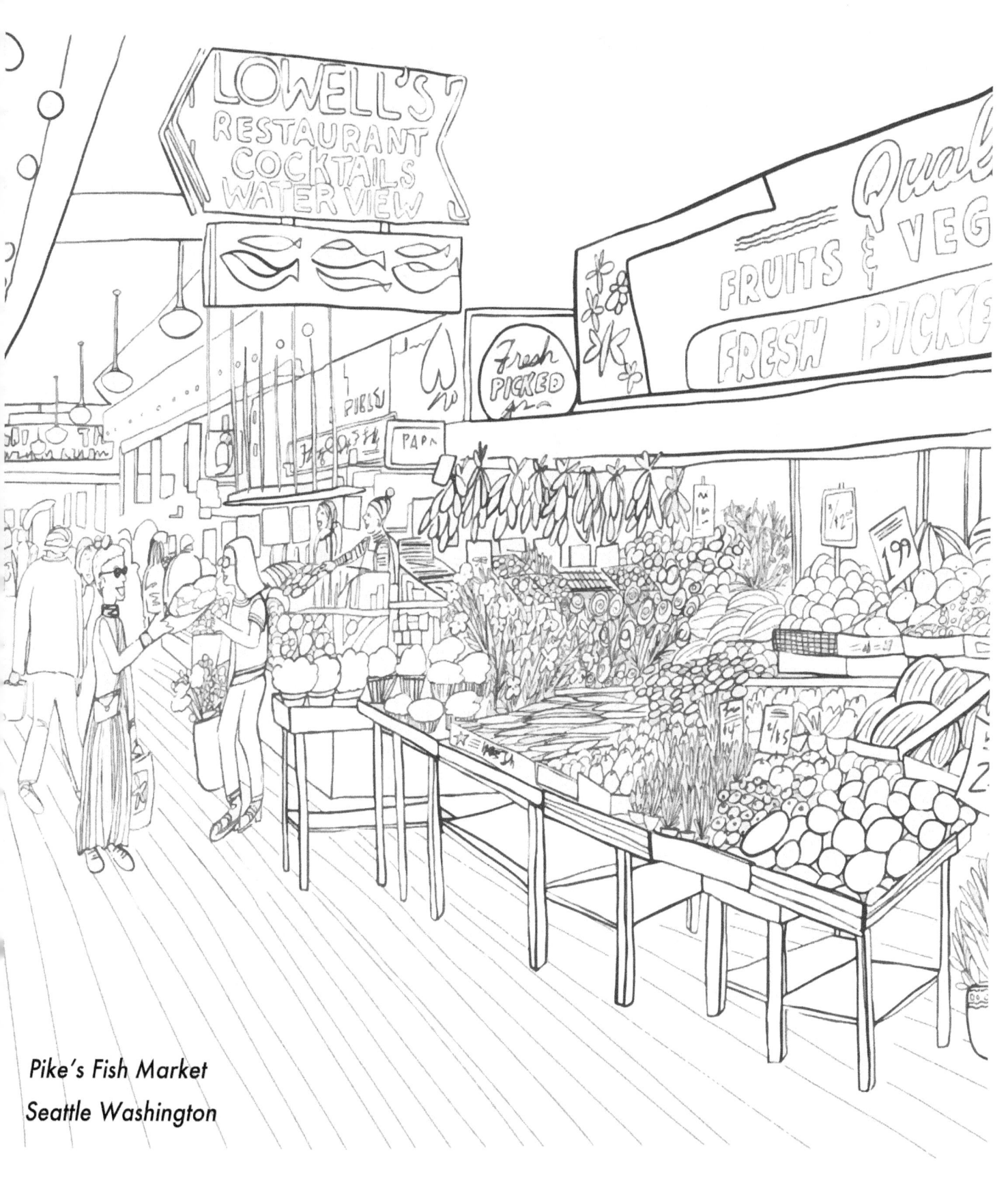

Pike's Fish Market
Seattle Washington

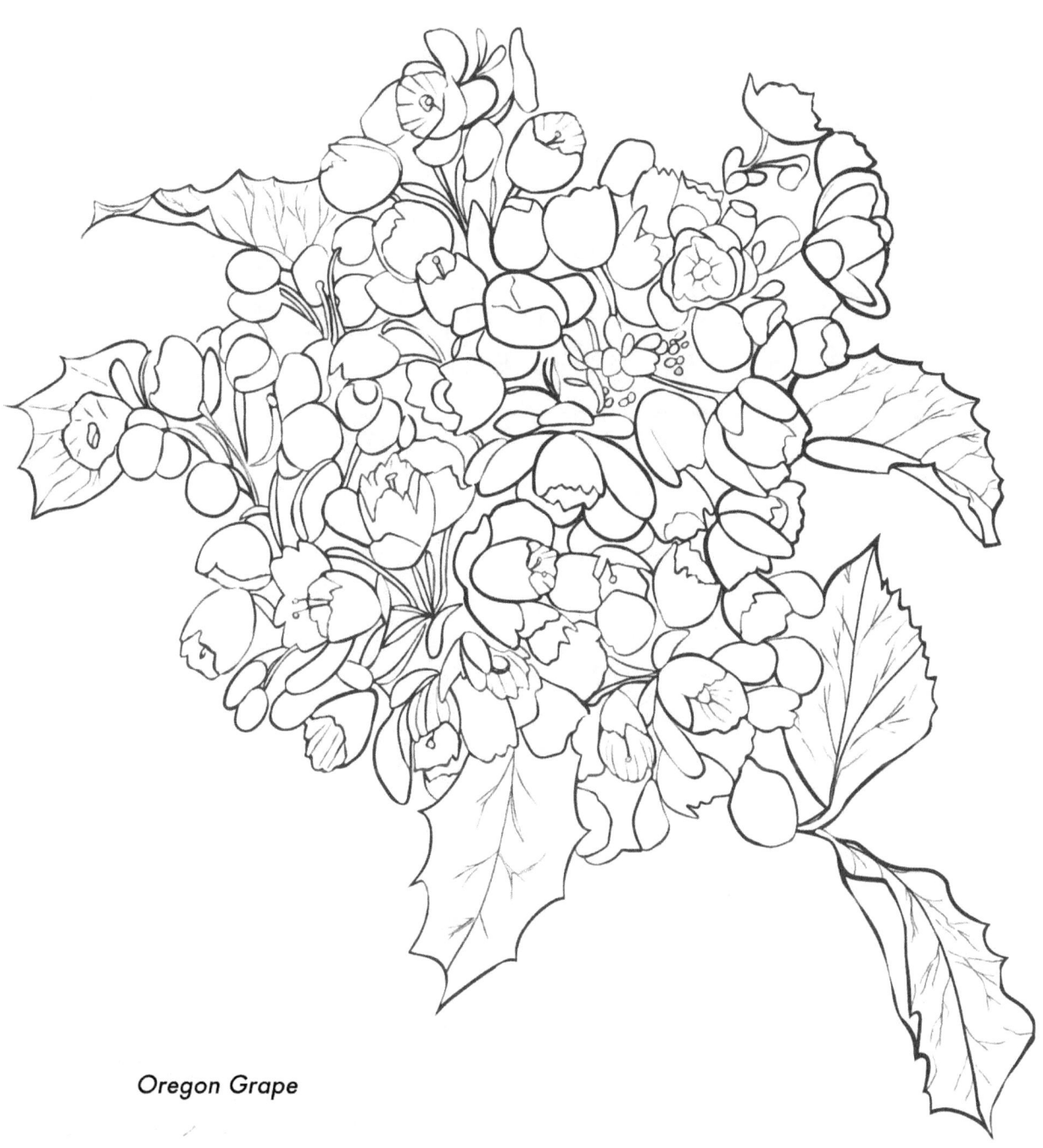

Oregon Grape

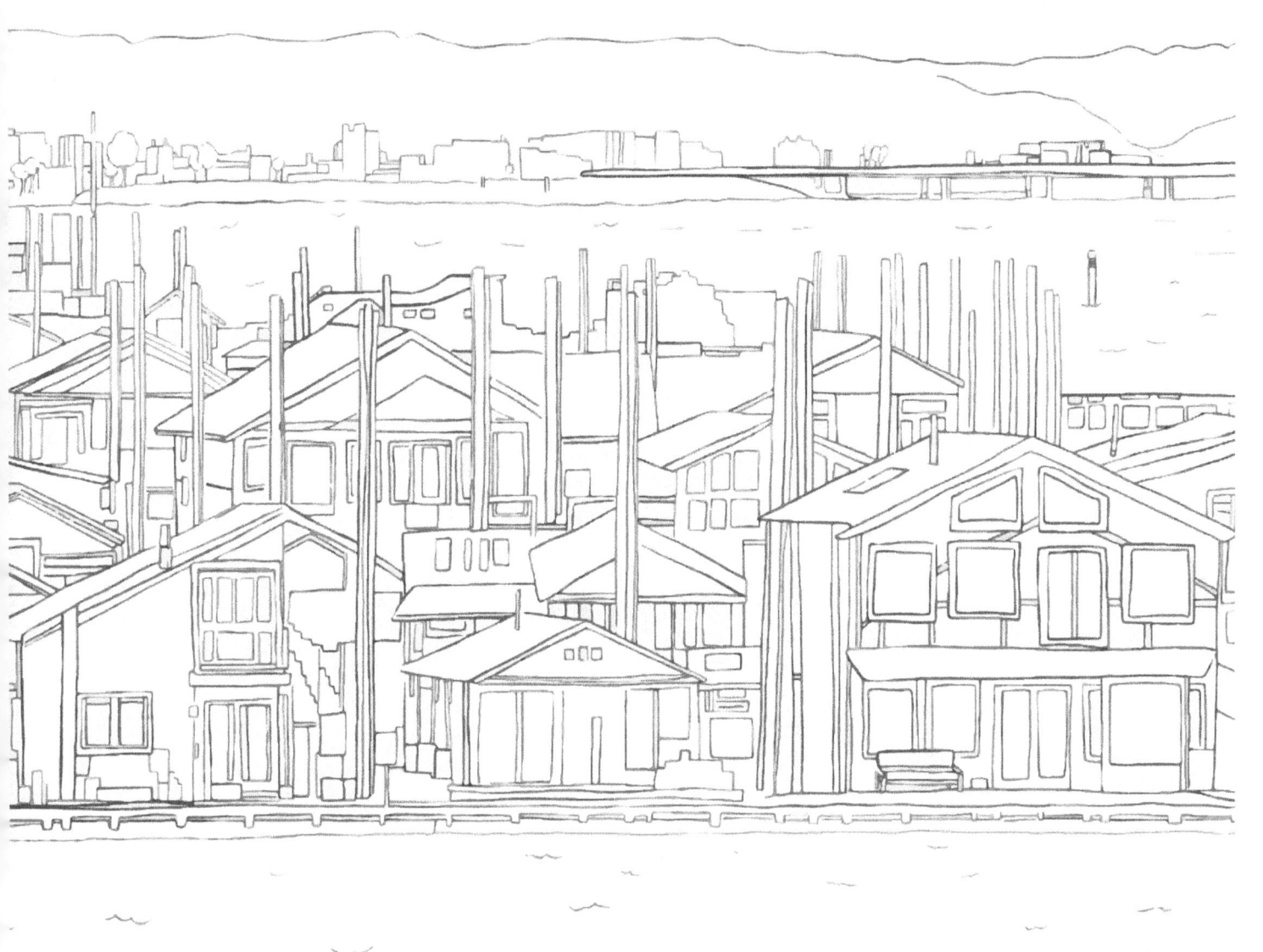

Portland Oregon

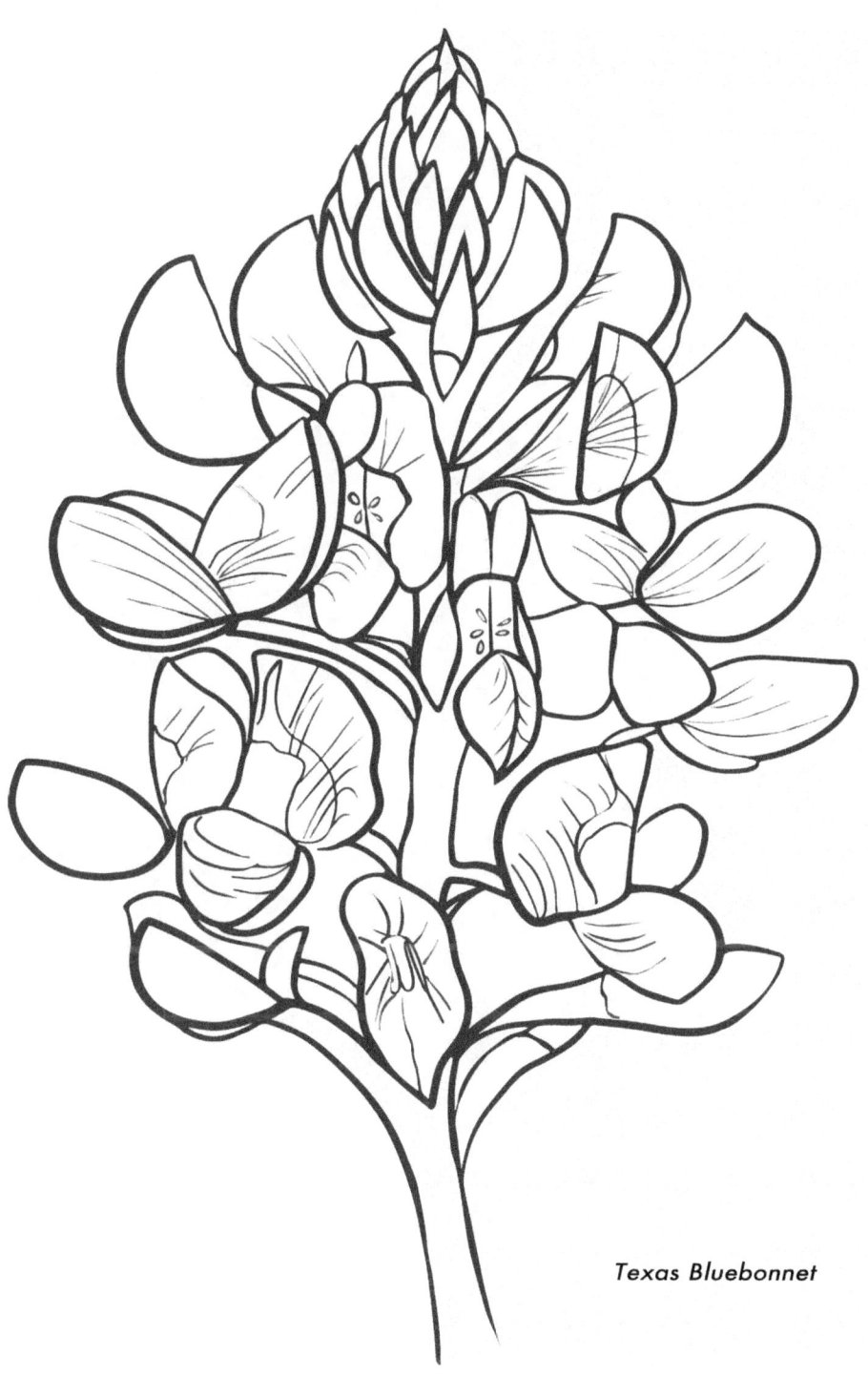

Texas Bluebonnet

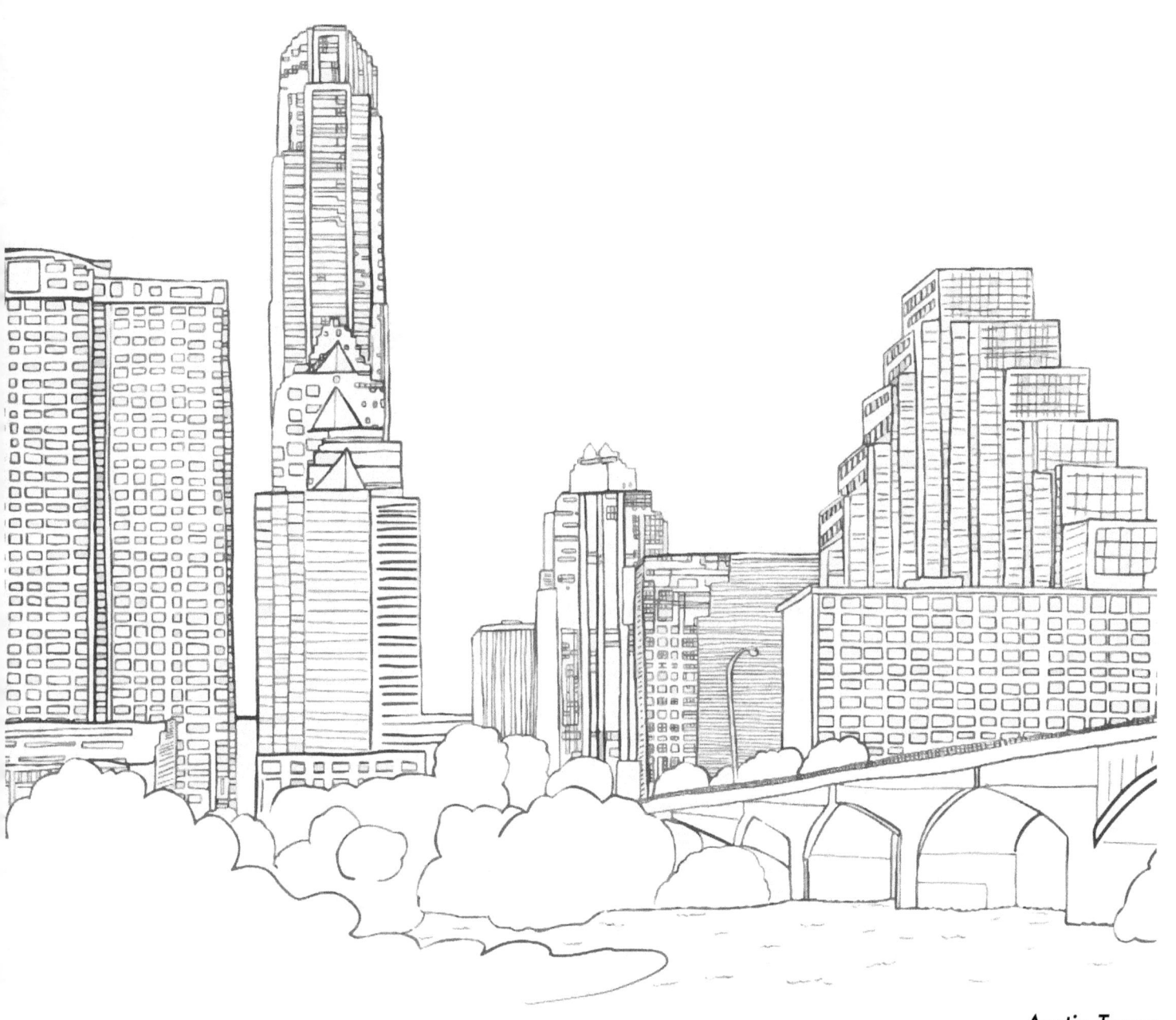

Austin Texas

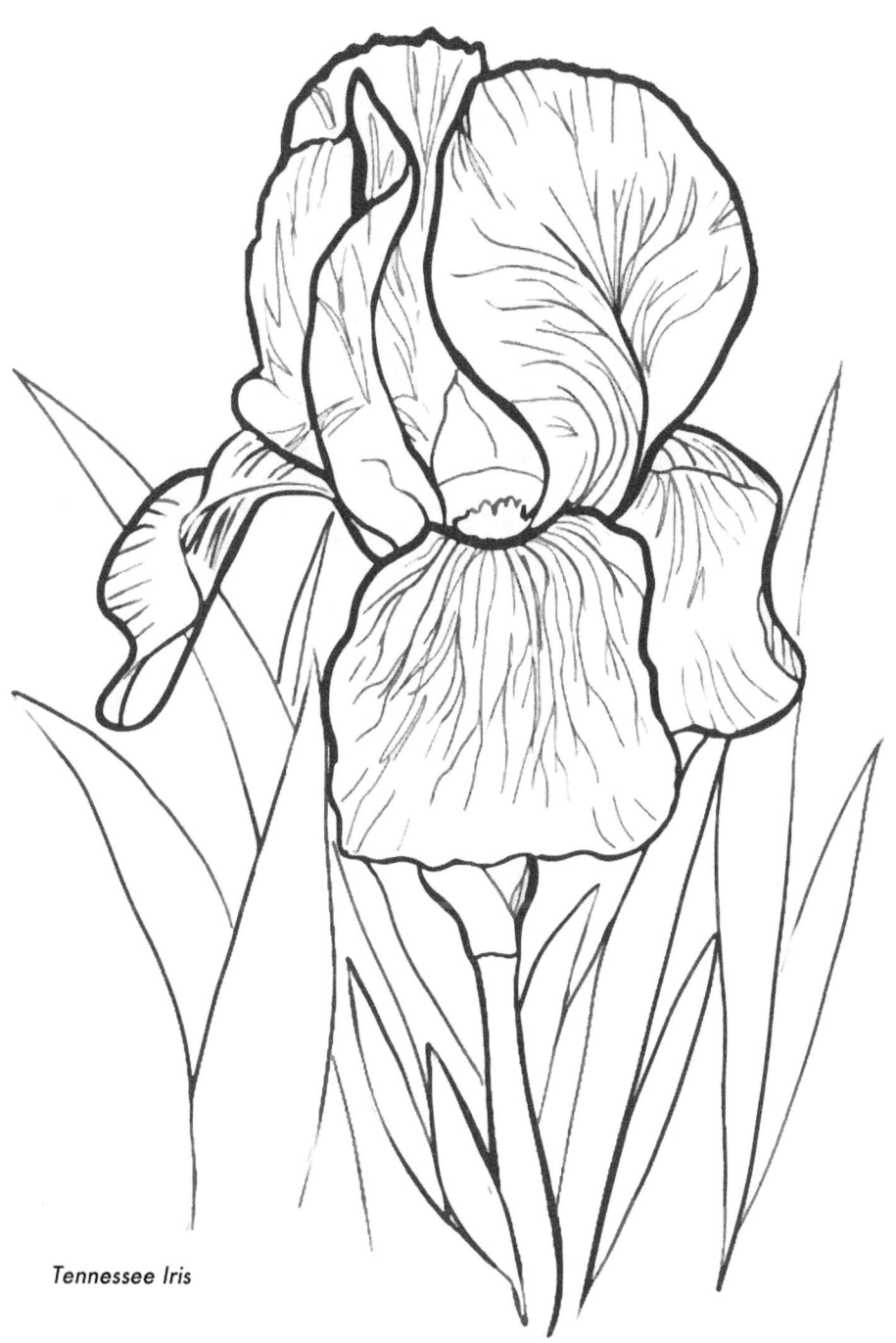

Tennessee Iris

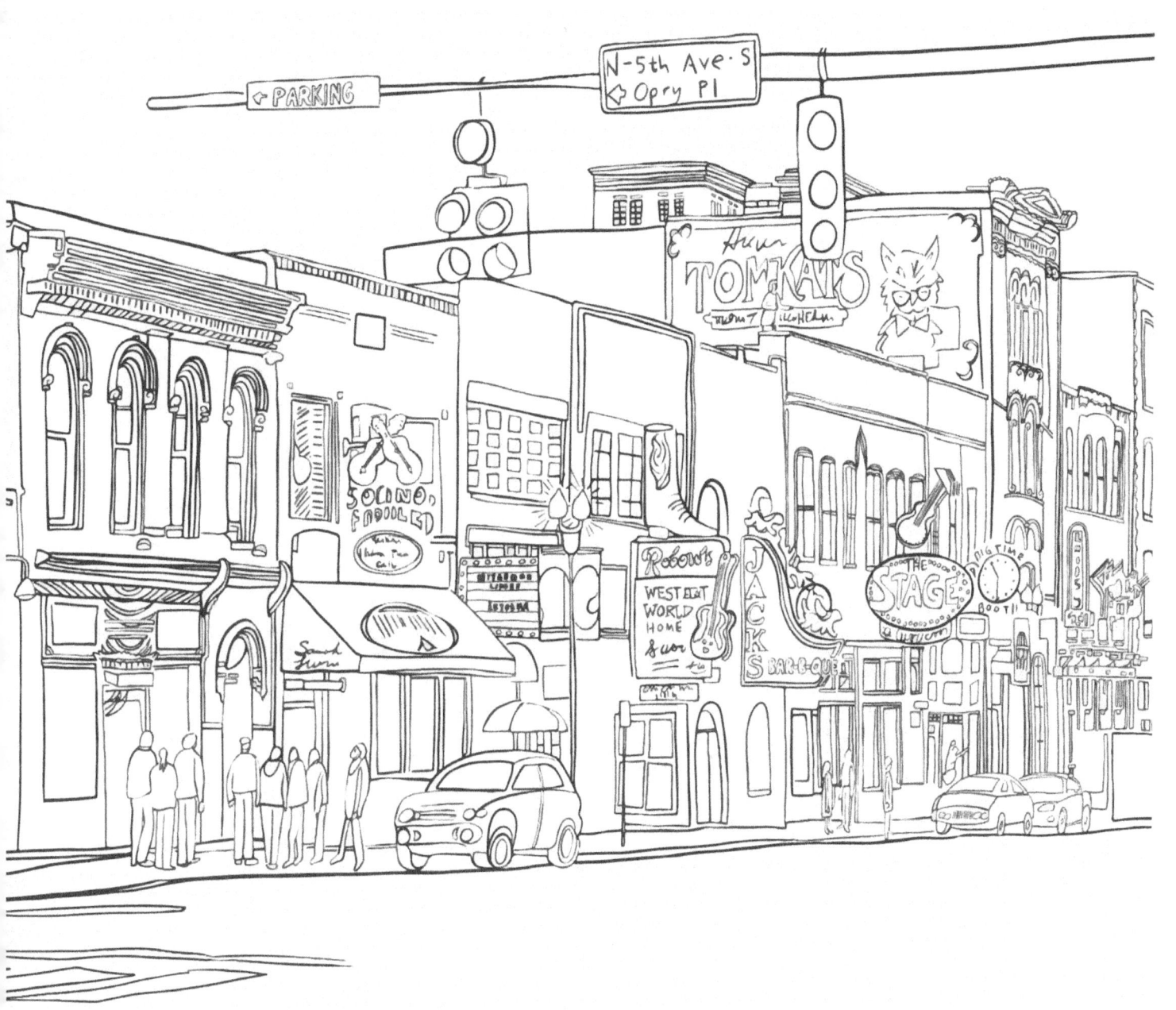

Nashville Tennessee

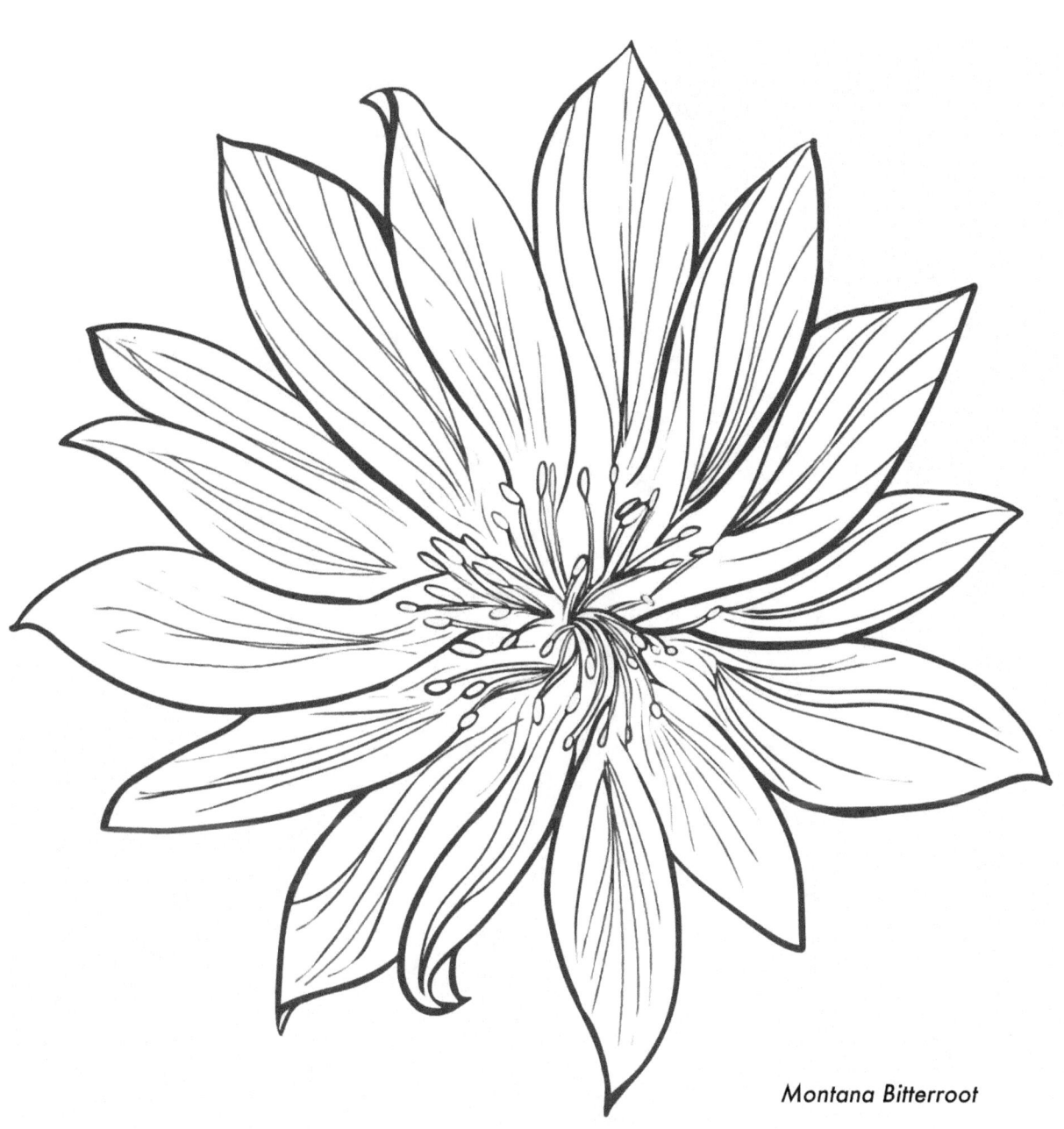

Montana Bitterroot

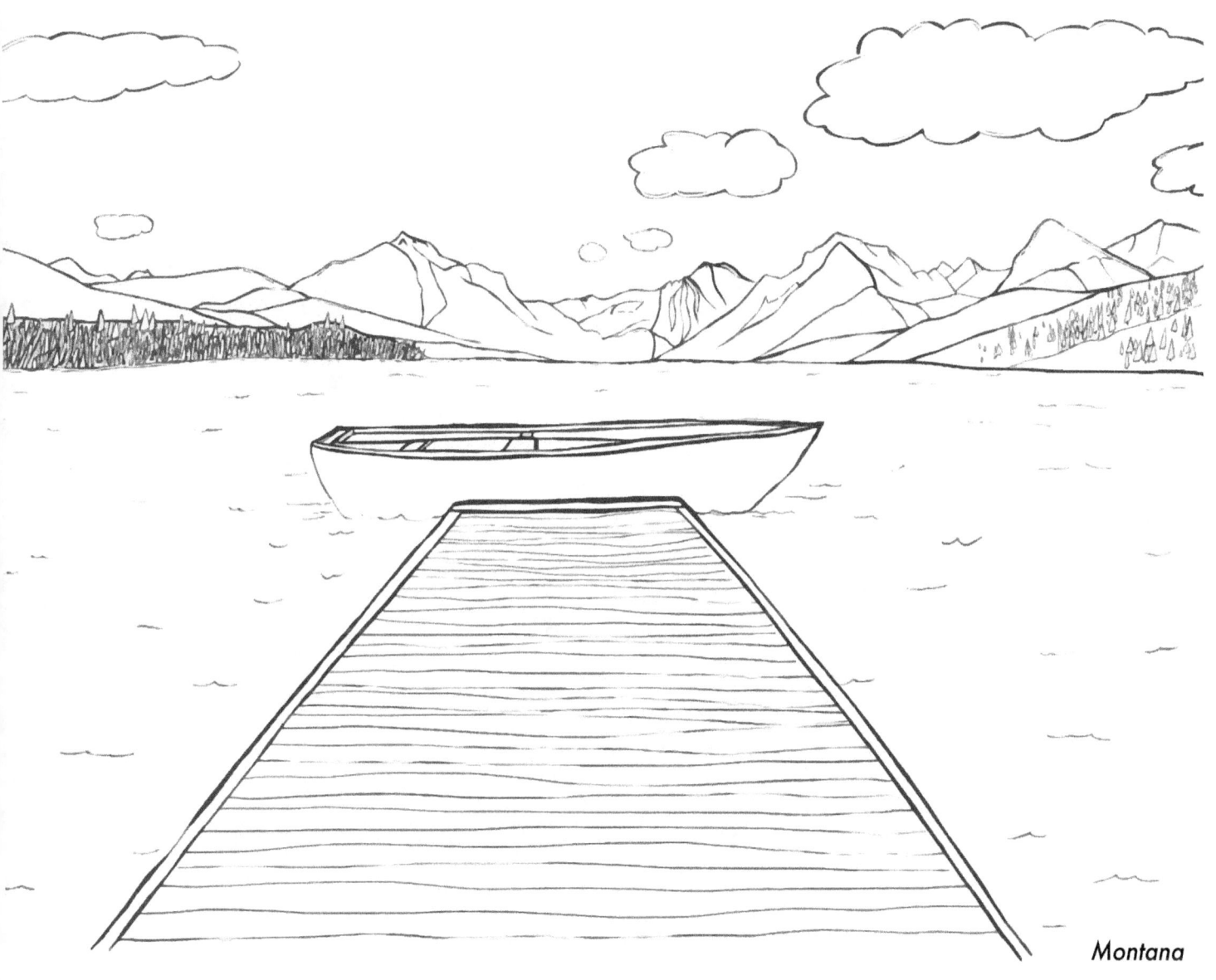

Montana

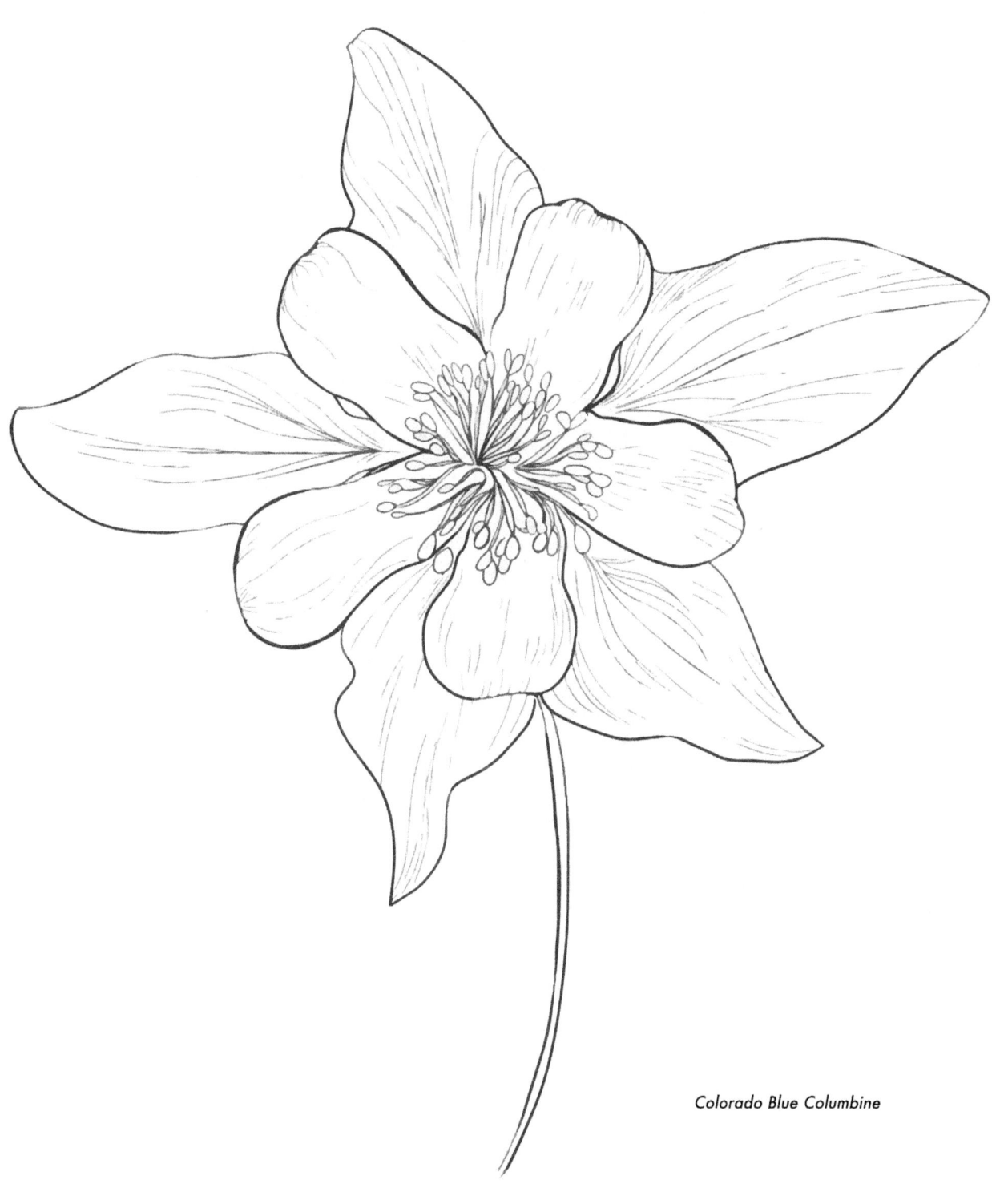

Colorado Blue Columbine

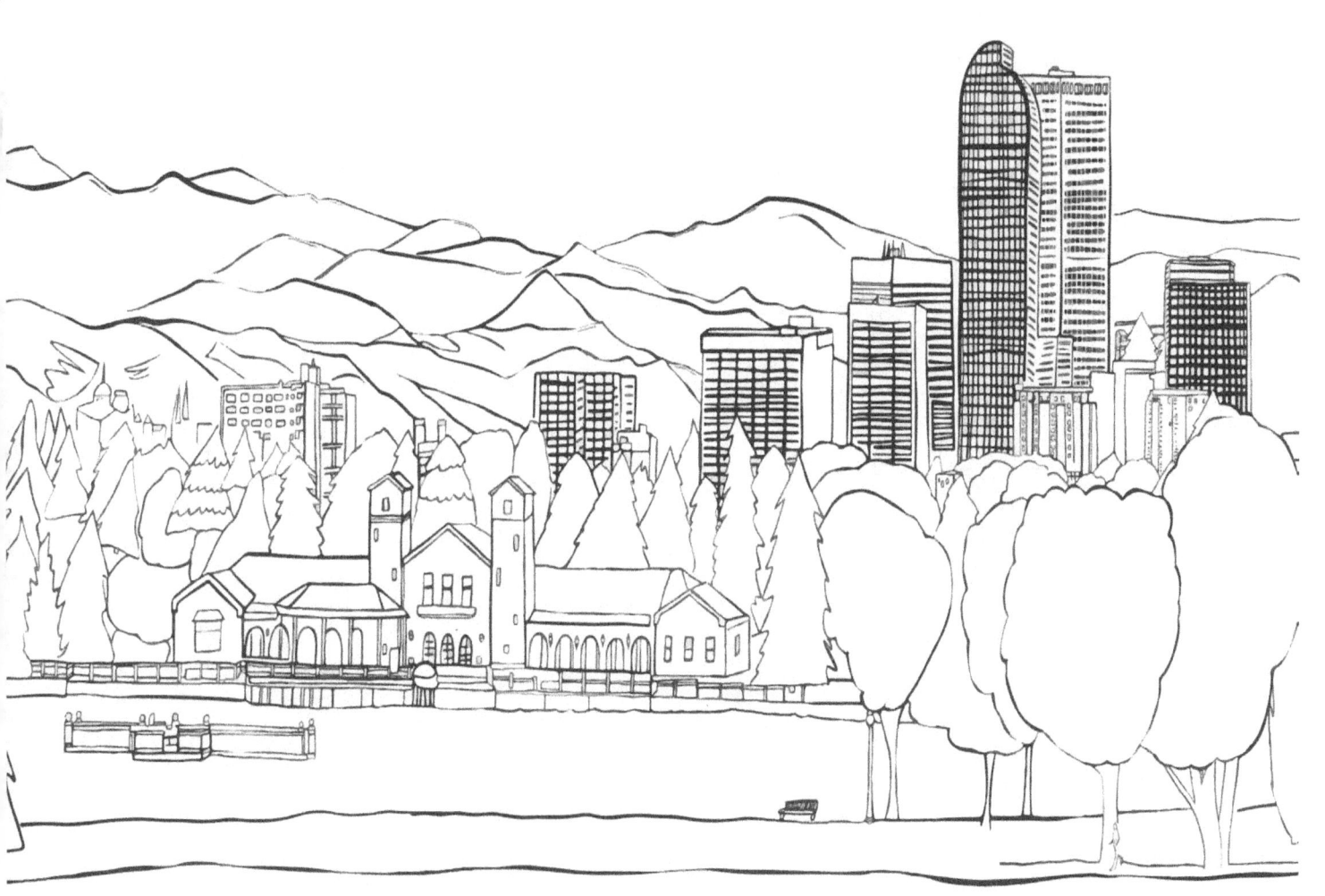

Denver Colorado

www.ingramcontent.com/pod-product-compliance
Lightning Source LLC
Chambersburg PA
CBHW080721190526
45169CB00006B/2460